W9-BHU-460

God's Got Your Number

A **DOVE Christian Book** by Ken Gaub

Other fine titles from DOVE Christian Books:

Nicky Cruz

Devil on the Run
"Brothers & Sisters, We Have a Problem
Destined to Win
How to Fight Back

David Wilkerson

Wise Warning — compiled and edited by Nicky Cruz

Keith Wilkerson

Midnight Raiders
Nightlark, Runner
Twilight Rebels

Dan Wooding

Miracles in Sin City (with Howard Cooper)
Singing in the Dark (with Barry Taylor)

Dr. Robert Schuller & Dr. Paul Yonggi Cho

Expand Your Horizon: (How to Make Your Faith Work!) w
Reid, John Meares and Richard Halverson

Reinhard Bonnke

Plundering Hell to Populate Heaven: The Vision of Reinhard E

Benson Idahosa

Faith + Works = Success

Van Johnson with Lloyd Hildebrand

Tackle the Impossible!

David Edwards with David Hazard

The Joy of Intimacy

God's Got Your Number

by Ken Gaub

Youth Outreach Unlimited
P.O. Box 1
Yakima, WA 98907 USA
(509) 575-1965

DOVE Christian Books

Melbourne, Florida

GOD'S GOT YOUR NUMBER

Copyright © 1986, 1990 by Ken Gaub
ISBN 0-926557-38-6

*All rights reserved. No part of this book may be reproduced without permission f
publisher, except by a reviewer who may quote brief passages in a review; nor n
part of this book be reproduced, stored in a retrieval system or copied by mechc
photocopying, recording or other means, without permission from the publis*

*Harbour House Publishers of Fine Books, P.O. Box 36-0122, Melbourn
32936*

*Cover artwork by Richard Nakamoto • Editorial work and typographical de
Publications Technologies, Eau Gallie, Florida*
Printed in the United States of America

DOVE Christian Books are available from good bookstores worldwide. Con
DOVE Christian Publications, 1425 Aurora Road, Melbourne, FL 32935 US
special quantity discounts for bulk purchases for sales promotions, premiu
fund raising, evangelistic or educational use. Special books or book excerp
also be created to fit specific needs. For details write or telephone the Mark
Department, DOVE Christian Books, 1425 Aurora Road, Melbourne, FL 32S
(407) 242-8290.

DOVE Christian Books, Inc. is a member of the American Booksellers Association a
Christian Booksellers Association. DOVE Christian Books are distributed in the Uni
States by Spring Arbor, Riverside, Ingram, Baker & Taylor, Appalachian, Whitaker F
Choice Books, and the Zondervan Family Bookstores. Contact DOVE for informatioi
our international distributors in Canada, the United Kingdom, Australia, New Zealar
Singapore, India, South Africa, Hong Kong, Malaysia, the Philippines, Ghana, Nige
Finland, Colombia and Argentina.

CONTENTS

This book is dedicated to:
My wife, Barbara, who stood with me during the hardships of years on the road.

My parents, John and Millie Gaub, without whose support this ministry would not have survived.

My brother, Mike, and sisters, Shirley, Carol, Esther, and Ruth, who know my faults and love me anyway.

My children, Nathan, Daniel, and Rebekah, and members of *Illustrator*, formerly known as *Eternity Express*, who have put bringing others to Christ ahead of personal gain.

My office staff, board members, and personal friends who support this ministry.

Ken Gaub

FOREWORD

Ken Gaub, along with the other members of *Youth Outreach Unlimited*, has encompassed the globe to bring the hopeful message of the Gospel to a lost and hurting world. Through many years he has proven his faithfulness and commitment to the Lord Jesus Christ.

The story of Ken Gaub and his expanding ministry is told in this exciting and readable book. May it bless all who take time to read these pages filled with true stories that highlight the lovingkindness of a miracle-working God.

Dr. Robert H. Schuller

SPECIAL THANKS

For several years people have asked me to write about the serious and funny things that have happened to me in my travels all over the world. Sometime ago I crossed paths with Wanda Herman and renewed our friendship of previous years. Wanda has written and ghost written many books, and she encouraged me to write this one.

Wanda and her husband, John, spent many hours going over old issues of our "Faith In Action" magazine and other printed materials. We spent days together with a tape recorder recalling some of the events of my life.

Without Wanda's tireless efforts in sorting and transcribing all the materials, this book would never have come into being.

Gratefully,

Ken

Chapter One

GOD'S GOT YOUR NUMBER

God, sometimes I wonder if you really know where I am! I thought. A melancholy cloud of self-pity enshrouded my mind. My hands tensed their grip on the steering wheel, and I stared through the windshield of our bus. The endless ribbon of superhighway stretched before me as I recalled the last few days of our fast-paced existence. I seemed to have used up all my faith in ministering to others. Even my sense of humor was hollow.

God, even a preacher needs to know that you are aware of him once in a while, I pleaded inside.

"Hey, Dad. Let's get some pizza." The voice of my younger son Dan stirred me out of my self-induced cocoon of despondency. My wife Barbara and daughter Becki agreed with Dan. It had been a long day and was way past time to eat.

"Okay," I yelled back. A large, green sign loomed ahead. I flipped on my right turn signal and picked up the CB microphone to inform my oldest son Nathan of our plans to pull off the highway. He and his wife followed closely in in another bus.

We exited from I-75 and turned onto Route 741 just

south of Dayton, Ohio. Bright, colorful signs advertising a wide variety of fast food restaurants were a welcome sight. Satisfied murmurs arose behind me as we sighted the local pizza parlor.

As I maneuvered the big Silver Eagle bus into the parking lot, Dan and Becki were already clamoring to get out and into the restaurant. Even examining menus offered a diversion from the limited activities available inside our "home on wheels."

Barbara stood at the bottom step and turned to wait for me. I sat staring into space. "Aren't you coming, Ken?" she asked.

"Naw, I'm not really hungry," I replied. "You go ahead with the kids. I need to stretch out and unwind a bit."

"Okay, we'll be back soon," her voice trailed off.

I moved back into the living room area to the sofa, folded my arms behind my head, leaned back, and sighed. It really is a beautiful day, I thought as I glanced out the window. Maybe I should get some fresh air.

I stepped outside, closed the bus doors, and looked around. Noticing a Dairy Queen down the street, I thought, maybe I'm thirsty.

After purchasing a coke, I strolled in the direction of the bus, still musing about my feelings of God's apathy toward me. The impatient ringing of a telephone somewhere up the street jarred me out of my doldrums. It was coming from a phone booth at a service station on the corner. As I approached, I heard the phone continuing its unanswered *Ring! Ring! Ring!*

I paused and looked to see if anyone was going to answer the phone. Noise from the traffic flowing through the busy intersection must have drowned out the sound because the service station attendant continued looking after his customers, oblivious to the incessant ringing.

Why doesn't someone answer that phone? I wondered. The ringing continued. I began reasoning, It may be important. What if it's an emergency?

I started to walk away, but curiosity overcame my indifference. I stepped inside the booth and picked up the phone. "Hello," I said casually and took a big sip of coke.

The operator whined, "Long distance call for Ken Gaub."

My eyes widened, and I almost choked on a chunk of ice from my coke. Swallowing hard, I said, *"You're crazy!"* Realizing I shouldn't speak to an operator like that, I added, "This can't be! I was just walking down the street, not bothering anyone, and the phone was ringing . . . ."

The operator ignored my crude explanation and asked once more, "Is Ken Gaub there? I have a long distance call for him."

It took a moment to gain control of my babblings, but I finally replied, "Yes, he is." Searching for a possible explanation, I suddenly had the answer. "I know what this is! I'm on *Candid Camera!*"

While trying to locate the hidden camera, I reached up and tried to smooth my hair. I wanted to look my best for all those millions of television viewers. Stepping outside the phone booth and looking quickly in every direction, the telephone cord nearly broke as I stretched it to its limit. I couldn't find a camera anywhere! Impatiently, the operator interrupted again.

"I have a long distance call for Ken Gaub, sir. Is he

there?''

Still shaken as well as perplexed, I asked, "How in the world can this be? How did you reach me here? I was walking down the street, not bothering anyone, the pay phone started ringing, and I decided to answer it." My voice grew louder in the excitement. "I just answered it on chance. You can't mean me. This is *impossible!*"

"Well," the operator asked, "*is* Mr. Gaub there or isn't he?" The tone of her voice convinced me the call was real and that her patience was at its limit.

I then replied, "Yes, he is. I'm he."

She was not convinced. "Are you sure?" she asked.

Flustered, I half-laughingly replied, "As far as I know at this point, I am."

To avoid any further disasters, I sat my coke down as I heard another voice say, "Yes, that's him, operator. I believe that's him!"

I listened dumbfounded to a strange voice identify herself. The caller blurted, "Ken Gaub, I'm Millie from Harrisburg, Pennsylvania. You don't know me, but I'm desperate. Please help me."

"What can I do for you?" I responded.

She began weeping. I waited until she had regained control, and then she continued, "I'm about to commit suicide, and I just finished writing a note. While writing it, I began to pray and tell God I really didn't want to do this. I suddenly remembered seeing you on television and thought if I could just talk to you, you could help me. I knew that was impossible because I didn't know how to reach you, and I didn't know anyone who could help me find you. I continued writing my suicide note because I could see no way out of my situation. As I wrote, numbers came to my mind, and I scribbled them down."

At this point she began weeping again, and I prayed silently for wisdom to help her.

She continued, "I looked at the numbers and thought, Wouldn't it be wonderful if I had a miracle from God, and He has given me Ken's phone number? I decided to try calling it. I figured it was worth the chance. It really was. I can't believe I'm talking to you. Are you in your office in California?"

I replied, "Lady, I don't *have* an office in California. My office is in Yakima, Washington."

A little surprised, she asked, "Oh, really, then where are you?"

"Don't you know?" I responded. "You made the call."

She explained, "But I don't even know what area I'm calling. I just dialed the number that I had on this paper."

I told her, "Ma'am, you won't believe this, but I'm in a phone booth in Dayton, Ohio!"

"Really?" she exclaimed, "well, what are you doing there?"

I kidded her gently, "Well, I'm answering the phone. It was ringing as I walked by, so I answered it."

Knowing this encounter could only have been arranged by God, I began to counsel the woman. As she told me of her despair and frustration, the presence of the Holy Spirit flooded the phone booth giving me words of wisdom beyond my ability. In a matter of moments, she prayed the sinner's prayer and met the One who would lead her out of her situation into a new life.

I walked away from that telephone booth with an electrifying sense of our heavenly Father's concern for each of His children. I was astounded as I thought of the astronomical odds of this happening. With all the millions of phones and innumerable combinations of numbers, only an all-knowing God could have caused that woman to call that number in that phone booth at that moment in time.

Forgetting my coke and nearly bursting with exhilaration, I bounded up the steps and into the bus. I wondered if my family would believe my story. Maybe I better not tell this, I thought; but I couldn't contain it. "Barb, you won't believe this! *God knows where I am!*"

God also knows where you are. No one is immune to life's many problems, but God knows about them and acts according to your faith. He knows where you are. Isaiah 43:2 says, "When thou passeth through the waters, I will be with thee; and through the rivers, they shall not overflow thee: when thou walkest through the fire, thou shall not be burned; neither shall the flame kindle upon thee."

Place yourself in your heavenly Father's hands. Concentrate on knowing His will for your life, and He will never forsake or forget you. He knows what you face spiritually, physically, emotionally, and financially. Because God cares, you can cast all your cares on Him.

Chapter Two

YOU CAN'T RUN FROM GOD

"God, if you'll save my wife and baby, I'll preach the gospel."

The vow that my father made on December 8, 1935—the day of my birth—was to affect the rest of my life. As the bells of a nearby church rang out the Sunday school hour, Mom slowly began to rally from the brink of death during childbirth. I was ushered into the world that Sunday morning, the firstborn son of an unsaved farmer. Several years passed, however, before my father kept his part of the bargain with God.

One of my aunts, Christina Bentz, began to pressure my folks. "Make good your vows! Give your heart to God," she would say.

But Dad and Mom shrugged Dad's promise when everything was going right. They made every attempt to avoid Aunt Christina, but she didn't give up easily.

Dad was a heavy smoker. Not wanting to encourage me to take up smoking, he tried to quit. Breaking the habit was hard, so he secretly chewed tobacco to overcome his craving for cigarettes. One day, while playing in the car, I discovered his pouch of Red Man under the front seat. Before I had a chance to try a "chaw,"

Dad caught me with it.

When Dad and Mom went to bed that night, Mom fell asleep, and Dad listened to the radio. He heard a preacher describe how bad your lungs look when you smoke. His answer to the problem was to "look up to Jesus."

Dad looked over at Mom to make sure she was asleep and then said, "God, if that preacher knows what he is talking about, show me what you can do." Dad immediately began to breathe easier. The next morning marked the end of his tobacco habit.

New Beginnings

"Millie, I want you to get packed. We're moving away from here," Dad told Mom one day after a frustrating encounter with my persistent aunt.

"Leaving Colorado! But why, John?" Mom was surprised by the sudden decision.

"I don't know about you, but I've had it with that sister of yours. She's about to drive me crazy trying to make me get religion. She keeps telling me I need to get prayed through."

"John, I will admit she is persistent, but are you sure you want to move? Where would we go?"

Mom and Dad had both been born in North Dakota, although his parents had originally migrated from Israel. My ancestors had been born one hundred miles from Jerusalem. Feeling there was a new opportunity in North Dakota, my grandparents had moved there.

"I think I would like to move to the state of Washington. I've heard there are jobs out there. Here I'm just barely surviving doing farm work. Besides, my sister and her husband are there!'' he said with a twinkle in his eye.

The next thing we knew we were on our way, loaded to capacity in Dad's '28 Chevy and pulling a fourteen-foot trailer. A restless four-year old, I barely squeezed into the last empty space.

Arriving in Yakima, Washington, we found a thriving town full of expectant people who, like us, were hoping for a new start in life. We also found very few places to live. The only place in town Dad could find compatible with our family size and income was across the street from a church. It happened to be an old-fashioned church that believed in loud, lively worship. He realized, to his dismay, that he had moved several states away from my aunt only to find a church full of people just like Christina right across the street!

Mom became very annoyed with the revival meetings because the noise of singing and praying kept her and Dad awake long hours each night. Having been raised in a conservative church, they were against emotionalism.

God remembered my father's vow, however, and used some tragic circumstances to change Dad's mind.

God's Faithfulness

While helping to construct a tunnel in the state of Washington, Dad was electrocuted with 11,000 volts of electricity. His fellow workmen rushed him from the smoke-filled tunnel to the hospital. On the way, he wavered between consciousness and unconsciousness.

The doctor's grim diagnosis was a shock to Mom.

He doubted that Dad would survive. If he lived at all, he would never walk again.

Although his hands, back, knee caps, thighs, and even his finger tips were burnt out, Dad miraculously recovered. The church across the street had prayed diligently for him, and Dad was able to walk out of the hospital just five days after the accident.

In spite of this miracle, my parents continued to have trouble in their marriage and at home. They were not getting along, and both felt like life was not worth living. Out of desperation, my parents decided to visit the little church across the street.

On January 1, 1939, Dad and Mom went to the church, stepped forward, and knelt by an old-fashioned altar to dedicate their lives to God. Mom received the Lord's forgiveness and salvation, but Dad had to go back again Wednesday night before he got the full assurance that all was okay in his life.

The Mead Avenue Church in Yakima, Washington, became the center of their existence. Although times were hard, they were sustained by the nurturing of the Word of God.

From that time, I began to see amazing miracles and answers to prayer in my parents' lives, and I knew it had to be because of their commitment to God. It wasn't always an easy road for my parents, but God promises in His Word that He honors the faith of the faithful. Blessings come through obedience. Jeremiah 7:23 says, ''But this thing commanded I them, saying, Obey my voice, and I will be your God, and ye shall be my people: and walk ye in all the ways that I have commanded you, that it may be well unto you.''

Dad kept his promise to preach. More than 40 years

later, Dad pastored the church on Mead Avenue where he found the Lord. All six of his children are serving God, and he finds particular enjoyment in working with our ministry. I Kings 3:14 says, "If thou wilt walk in my ways. . .then I will lengthen thy days." My father is living proof of this promise.

Rise Up And Walk

After Dad started his own equipment business in Yakima, he kept well occupied in the spring and summer months. In the winter, however, he had spare time to help around the church. On one occasion, he and several other men volunteered to fix a large crack in the basement of the parsonage, where leaking water was damaging the wall.

Dad began to build another wall to reinforce the original wall. While he was down on his knees preparing mortar for the work, he heard a crack. Suddenly, nine hundred pounds of concrete wall broke away and fell on top of him, pinning him to the gravel floor.

"My God, he'll be crushed!" one man cried.

"Get him out of there!" another yelled.

One of the other men just stared and burst into tears. "You know it's too late. He's dead by now. That wall got him instantly."

Nevertheless, several men began to work frantically to lift the wall off Dad. After getting it braced, they found Dad lying, broken and crushed under the rubble. By removing the basement door from its hinges, the men made a makeshift stretcher and maneuvered him onto it.

At the same time, something miraculous was happening in Dad's spirit. In his semi-conscious state, he heard a voice say, "Rise up and walk."

Thinking he was speaking aloud, Dad responded, "Lord, I can't!"

All that the men heard was a moan. They were startled. "Let's hurry! He's still alive!"

Dad passed into unconsciousness again. Shortly, the pain roused him once more. "Rise and walk!" the voice again urged.

Again he replied, "Lord, I can't!"

By this time the men were making their way up the basement steps, intending to rush him to a hospital.

The voice urged a third time. "Rise and walk!" At that moment, a mighty flow of God's presence swept over Dad. Strength pulsated through his body. He sat up, raised his hands, and began shouting, "Praise the Lord! Praise the Lord!"

The men struggled to hold him because they were convinced he was suffering from shock. With the strength of Samson, he pushed them aside and got up. "I'm fine! I'm healed!" he yelled. "Look at me!"

He began praising the Lord, and soon the other men joined in. Upon examination the next day, Dad didn't even have a bruise, and he went back to work. Needless to say, a spirit of revival began in the church as Dad testified to God's miraculous power.

My parents' faith was tested at other times, but they always responded with prayer and simple trust in God.

Chapter Three

FAITH OF OUR FATHERS

We moved from Washington to Oregon to pastor a church where one day I and two other little boys gave our lives to Jesus after an altar call by my uncle, the Rev. David Gaub. He will share in the reward for all those who have found Christ through our ministry.

Then we moved to Fertile, Iowa, near the Minnesota border where we lacked indoor plumbing, making Saturday night baths a comedy. We had running water, but *I* was the one who had to run to draw it! After lathering up, we kids stood under a bucket with a nozzle. We hurried since there was only enough water in the bucket to rinse all the soap off.

In our home, we children understood that Dad's word was law. Fear, coupled with the respect I held for him, kept me out of a lot of mischief..

One day Dad shared with me, "Son, I want to be **good example for you especially now that your mother and I are serving the Lord.''**

Because of my admiration for Dad, I began to emulate him in his every mannerism. Mom would laugh when she saw me trying to be like Dad even in the way he walked.

The Divine Mechanic

After moving to Iowa, perhaps the miracle that remains most vivid in my memory involves my Dad's old

Mercury. During revival meetings, Dad had been driving the car to and from the church he pastored. The guest evangelist was having a tremendous meeting, and many people were being saved and healed. Although the financial needs of the evangelist were being met, the congregation had forgotten that the pastor and his family needed support.

Toward the end of the revival meetings, Dad came home discouraged. The old car had barely made it to and from church that evening.

As he lay in bed that night, Dad began to pray, "Lord, this is it. It costs a dollar just to go back and forth to church each night. I've used every dime I've got and given everything I have to the ministry. I can't charge gas because I wouldn't have the money to pay the bill when it came.

"Besides, Lord, the car has gone its last mile. I've fixed every part I can fix. It's conked out and now won't even start. I barely made it home tonight. The car needs a valve job, and you know I can't afford that either. Lord, this will just have to be my last night to go to church. I guess we'll have to beg. . . ."

After tossing, turning, and worrying for a long time, Dad fell into a deep sleep and began to dream. He saw himself walking out to the car and noticed a light shining around it. That's strange, he said to himself. How can there be light at night?

Going to the car, he saw that the hood was up. The glow of light was not coming from natural light but emanated from all around the car. As he walked to the front, he was surprised to find someone bent over the car apparently working on it. The most startling discovery was that the mechanic radiated the light. It was Jesus!

Dad woke with a start, amazed to find himself still in bed. The scene had been so real that he went quickly to the window to check on the car. He saw no light. Throwing on some clothes, he ran outside and cautiously approached the car. No one was under the hood, but his pulse quickened with anticipation.

Expectantly, he got into the car and turned the ignition key. The engine roared to life, and Dad noticed no pinging, clanging, smoking, or choking. *The engine ran smoothly.*

That morning at breakfast, Dad told the family about his dream and the mechanical miracle. To test it out, Dad drove my sisters and I to school. That test drive proved to me that nothing was impossible. If Jesus could fix the old Mercury, He could do anything.

Preacher Or Comedian?

Growing up as a preacher's kid wasn't easy. I tried hard to live right, but the boy in me wanted to enjoy life. A constant struggle between the good little minister's son and the ornery preacher's kid raged inside me.

When I was being "good," I wanted to be a preacher. I would practice preaching "hell, fire, and brimstone" sermons to our chickens and then give an altar call. As a child, I really believed that a lot of those chickens got saved!

When I was fourteen, I found work in the spring and summer driving a tractor for neighboring farmers. The normal speed for a tractor is three miles per hour, but I thought that was too slow. When the farmer wasn't looking, I'd put the tractor into road gear—about fifteen miles per hour—and the job wasn't nearly as boring. If I made one little deviation at that speed, however, I'd take out whole rows of corn before I could bring the tractor back under control.

My main purpose for hurrying was to gain extra time to practice preaching in the back field. I would shove the throttle into road gear down a row, slow down on the turn at the edge of the field, whip the tractor around, and start with a roar back up the other side. After about two hours of fast, furious plowing, I gained extra time to ''preach'' to the corn, the fence, and the trees.

I would see corn stalks with their tassels waving in the breeze and say, ''They're praising the Lord.''

Although Mom and Dad expected me to be a preacher, I wanted to be a comedian. I was torn between the two. In private, I ''preached'' but kept my call between God and me. In public, I acted like a clown. It made me feel good to see people laugh, and I tried to be the life of every party, stealing the show with my antics and comic remarks.

My dilemma was to figure out how I could be a comedian, do what I wanted to do, and still satisfy God and my parents. Unfortunately, this longing for excitement almost got me into a lot of trouble.

Indulging In Sin

Going home from school one day, a friend of mine and I found a six-pack of unopened beer bottles alongside the road. Here is an opportunity to do something really sinful, I thought. ''Hey, Bob, why don't we haul off and get drunk?'' I figured that if I really got drunk, I would be too much of a sinner for God to call me to preach.

Bob thought it was a good idea, and we found a clump of bushes where no one could see us.

"Hey, Ken, let's see if we can blow the tops off these things," Bob laughed and began shaking one of the bottles vigorously.

"Give me one," I said, jerking it from his hand. I pried off the top, and warm beer spewed everywhere. We were both drenched. Foam ran down our faces, our hair was soaked, and our clothes smelled horrible.

"Ken," Bob said, grinning impishly, "we might as well drink this stuff. The way we smell we're going to get accused anyway."

The smell was repugnant, and I wasn't sure this was what I wanted to do after all. Bob opened one of the other bottles and started drinking. "Come on, chicken," he teased as I half-heartedly tried to remove the cap.

Placing the bottle to my lips, I pretended to drink. As Bob drank three or four more beers, I acted like I was drunk. In a short while, Bob got sick and laid down on the grass. I made a decision then that any sinning I did in the future would *not* include drinking.

Somehow, my folks never found out about the beer party. But that wasn't the end of my misadventures.

It was hard to find something sinful to do because Dad's strict ten o'clock curfew didn't give me much time. When all the other boys were just getting started, I always had to go home. And ten o'clock meant exactly that, not one minute after ten. If I came home at 10:05, I might as well stay out all night—I got the same punishment.

Since I had little opportunity to be a *real* sinner around home, another buddy and I decided to go on a fishing trip. On our way, I informed him of my plan. "While we're gone, we're going to be worldly. No one will know what we're doing. Let's be as mean as the devil."

Bob and I both came from conservative Midwest families, so we had led very sheltered lives. The most sinful thing we could think of was to smoke cigars. Fearing someone would see us buy them and tell Dad, we stole them.

After arriving at our fishing site, we baited our hooks and cast in our lines. We then set our poles so we could watch the bobbers and with much ceremony took out the first cigar. After removing the cellophane wrapper, I bit off the tip and handed it to my pal. He lit it, and we took turns taking big puffs, inhaling as much as possible and coughing considerably between puffs.

The air around us became a smoky white haze. Within a few minutes we had finished off the first cigar, and soon I began feeling a little dizzy. The next "stogie" wasn't even half gone when we both became sick. We just lay beside the river feeling like we were going to die. Catching fish was the furthest thing from our minds. Trying to be a sinner wasn't as easy as I had imagined.

Proverbs 13:15 says, "The way of the transgressor is hard." But Jesus states that His "yoke is easy" and His "burden is light" (Matthew 11:30). Many people don't realize how often God protects them and takes care of them—even before they know Him.

My parents taught me the right way. As Solomon said

in Proverbs, "Train up a child in the way he should go, and when he is old, he will not depart from it" (22:6). This doesn't mean he won't wander, run astray, or cause heartache, but the promise is that he will return. I am living proof.

Chapter Four

SOMEDAY

"Hey, Ken, where are you going so fast?" yelled one of my buddies as I whizzed past a group of them loitering on the school steps. On any other spring day I would have joined the guys in their after-school horseplay.

"Hey, ain't you heard? There's a man down at Des Moines that's saving people and healing them. He's got a tent bigger than anything you have ever seen, and *we're* going to see him," I boasted. A trip anywhere was an adventure to a young son of a poor preacher.

"Wow! That's great!" exclaimed another of the boys.

"Yeah! They're holding the meeting right on the lawn of the capitol. Dad said the preacher couldn't get a permit to put the big tent up anywhere else, so the Governor told him he could use the capitol lawn. Can't you just see that? Those big tent stakes going right down in that grass they keep smooth as a carpet. Whoosh!" Swinging my arms, I pounded imaginary stakes into the ground to the amusement of my friends.

"Boy, I wish I could see a tent that big!" one friend said.

"Me, too!" chimed in another.

"Yeah, well, I gotta go. Mom told me not to be late."
I fairly flew home, filled with pride at being the envy
of my peers; and, too, I could hardly wait to get to the
state capitol to see the big tent I'd heard about.

Since it was not my nature to be patient, the trip
downstate seemed unending. I tried to watch the passing scenery, but after awhile all the farms, with their
freshly plowed fields looking like acres of brown cor-
duroy, began to grow monotonous. My boredom was
infectious to the others in the cramped car. "Are we
almost there?" asked my younger sisters at least a dozen
times. Each time they were answered with a cheerful
but somewhat strained, "Not yet, honey. It won't be
much longer."

The sun was nearly setting when we finally arrived
in Des Moines. The capitol grounds and an area for
blocks around bustled with activity. Cars lined every
available inch of curbed parking space. People jostled
one another on the sidewalks as they hurried past,
seemingly oblivious to the appealing displays in store
windows along the way. Everyone headed toward the
capitol building.

When Dad finally found a place to park the car, I
opened the door before the motor stopped running.
The others clamored out, and we joined the moving
mass of humanity.

The great tent was visible for several blocks. As we
approached, I was awestruck. It seemed so gigantic you
could almost set the capitol building inside. The pen-
nants atop the poles and the noisy people milling about
created an almost carnival-like atmosphere.

We walked past a gleaming tractor trailer rig. On the
lower portion of the trailer, near the front and in

modest-sized letters, were the words, "Oral Roberts Evangelistic Association, Tulsa, Oklahoma."

Entering the cavernous tent, I was equally amazed by its interior proportions. Thousands of metal folding chairs in neat rows formed a semi-circle facing the platform. Immediately in front of the podium, a walkway with ramps rose from either side. A huge sign hanging on the rear wall said, "Expect A Miracle."

Whole sections of chairs near the back were still empty; but at the rate people were pouring in, I knew the tent would soon be full. As they moved through the tent, their feet stirred the sawdust that carpeted the ground. The smell of freshly cut wood permeated the air, and overhead lights shone through a haze of dust.

I was captivated by the size of the huge center poles that thrust through the peaks of the tent roof. To my young mind, they looked a hundred feet tall.

The Voice Of God

Service time was nearly an hour away, so after finding seats near the front, Mom said I could look around. Scuffing through the ankle-deep shavings, I ambled outside.

Craning my neck to study every angle, I wandered around the outer perimeter of the tawny mountain of canvas. I tugged on the thick ropes tied to huge stakes. The ropes were stretched tightly to huge center support poles on which the whole weight of the canvas rested. My mind was boggled by the yards of canvas required to make such a tent.

God surely must be with this man, I thought, otherwise there would be no way he could do something

33

like this and have these people come just to hear him preach.

In that hallowed moment, the desire to preach the gospel superseded all other earthly ambitions. How I could do it and still be funny was something that would have to be resolved; but at that point in time, becoming a preacher meant everything to me.

Boy, if one person can set up a tent like this in the state capitol and have thousands of people come to see him . . . and the Governor of the state would let him do it . . . my thoughts ran rampant.

I swung under one of the strong tautly stretched tent ropes. God can do anything, I said to myself.

No sooner had those words crossed my mind when I heard the words, *"I can!"*

Instantly, I knew it was the voice of God. He had actually spoken to me. Keenly aware of the sacredness of what was happening, I didn't want to run from it.

The voice had spoken so loudly that everyone nearby should have heard it. Yet, no one else in view seemed aware of the words I had heard.

After joining my parents inside the tent, I sat in quiet introspection until the evening service began. The presence of God felt very real to me that night. As Oral Roberts spoke, I hung onto every word. It seemed as though the sermon was for me alone. Yet the thousands of men, women, and children in that great tent cathedral were as equally moved as I.

Reverend Roberts preached a simple but powerful message. The atmosphere was charged with faith, and hundreds responded to the invitation to "believe on the Lord Jesus Christ" for forgiveness of sins. After those seeking salvation prayed the "sinner's prayer" of repentance, they were ushered to a special prayer tent for counseling.

A line then formed to the right of the platform for those who needed healing. In shirtsleeves, and with his tie hung loosely about his open collar, Oral Roberts prayed for the sick. He sat on a folding chair at the edge of the platform, and a microphone stood beside him. Laying both hands on the head of the sick person, he prayed "in the name of Jesus Christ of Nazareth" that they would be healed. He raised his eyes toward the ceiling as though looking into the face of Jesus. The sincerity etched into his American Indian features was unmistakable. I watched every move.

By the time he prayed for the last needy person, Oral Roberts' shirt was drenched with perspiration, and his coal black hair lay soaked against his head with one unruly strand hanging limply in front of his eyes. Miracle after miracle took place on the walkway in front of the platform. The sick, crippled, deaf, and blind came up one ramp and walked down the other ramp completely well and rejoicing.

When the benediction brought the service to its conclusion, I felt disappointed. I didn't want it to end. Staring toward the platform, I sat transfixed, rerunning through my mind the miracles I had witnessed minutes before.

The clamor of voices and the clanging of chairs broke the solemnity of the moment as ten thousand people shuffled toward the exits. Our family joined them and stepped out of the tent into the night.

My sisters fell asleep almost before we left the Des Moines city limits. On the long ride home, Dad and Mom talked excitedly about the demonstrations of the power of God through His servant, Oral Roberts. Sitting in silence in the back seat, I felt too emotionally full to speak. Tears flooded my eyes and trickled down my face. I recalled the night I had knelt at the altar in Uncle Dave Gaub's church when, laying his hand on my head, he prayed, "God, use this boy in gospel work all over the world."

Mom noticed my remoteness and asked, "Are you okay, Ken?"

Leaning forward in the darkness to rest my folded arms on the back of the driver's seat, I boldly stated, "Someday I'm going to do like that preacher. I'm going to have a tent and preach, and I'm going to help people just like Oral Roberts."

It has always been my goal to help those who are hurting and to lift them up—spiritually, physically, emotionally, and even financially. The Bible says, "Where there is no vision, the people perish" (Proverbs 29:18). Many people need just a little boost and I want to influence their lives in a positive way, showing them how to turn negatives into positives.

After many years, I am seeing people I have inspired coming to me with their own ministry. A policeman who found the Lord is now the director of his own ministry; a young man from New York who got turned on to Jesus now leads a Christian comedy group that reaches many kids in the Northeast; a nightclub owner is now a pastor; a drug addict has become a missionary; a kid from Arkansas found the Lord and is now the drummer of a well-known Christian band. Many others are now in Bible schools preparing themselves for different kinds of ministries.

These people were blessed through my ministry; I

was inspired by Rev. Roberts; and as a sick child, Oral Roberts was touched by another evangelist. We won't know all the results until we get to heaven. But it's easy to see how important planting seeds is. I encourage you to plant some seeds into hurting hearts that are ripe for the gospel of Jesus Christ. The harvest will yield eternal fruit.

Chapter Five

THE WHITE BIBLE

Nearly three years had passed since the Oral Roberts crusade in Des Moines, Iowa. Although the memory of that night was indelibly imprinted upon my mind, the encounter with the voice of God did not guarantee instant sainthood. The glitter and glamour of Hollywood still beckoned, and the desire to be a comedian still dominated my fantasies and dreams.

One evening I returned home completely exhausted from my part-time job at a grocery store in nearby Mason City. Not only was I physically weary from going to school and working but I was still struggling to find direction for my life.

After supper, I excused myself from the table and announced, "I don't think I'll go to church tonight."

Dad raised his eyebrows and stared sternly at me. "Now, Kenneth, you know how we feel about people staying home from church. Everyone in this house goes to church when it's church time. Bad things might happen if you stay home."

"But, Dad," I sighed, "I'm not going to do anything. I really just want to rest. Look, if it will make you feel better, you can leave the girls here with me."

For me to offer to take care of my sisters, Shirley, Carol, Esther, and Ruth, was unheard of. At first, my parents looked puzzled. But the look on my face must have convinced them that my plans were not of a mischievous nature.

Having noticed my downcast expression throughout the evening meal, Mom sensed my anxiety. "John," she said, "maybe it won't hurt to let Ken stay home just this one time. It looks as though he's got things to sort out in his mind. I don't think it would hurt to let him stay here and watch the girls."

My sisters were delighted at the opportunity to stay at home, but getting them to bed was a hassle. After settling the last argument, I finally got them into their rooms and quieted down for the night.

Relieved that I could finally be alone, I headed to my room. Tense and wound up like the mainspring of a watch, I stretched across the bed. Suddenly I heard a knock at the front door.

Oh, no! Who can that be? I wondered. Wouldn't you know it? Finally, I have a few minutes to myself, I am ready to relax, and someone picks this time to visit.

I hurried downstairs to answer the door, but to my amazement no one was there! Poking my head outside and peering about, I didn't see a soul. Must have been my imagination, I thought. As I started back up the steps, the insistent rapping began again. I paused on the landing, thinking maybe the wind was blowing a tree limb against the house. But no, the knocking was coming from the direction of the front door.

Believing that whoever had knocked the first time must have just walked away for a minute, I decided to answer the door again. I discovered an empty porch once again. Wanting to make sure it was not someone playing a prank, I stepped outside for a better look. Something strange was happening, and I wasn't quite sure what.

When my search proved unfruitful, I ran back inside the house. A bit shaken, I slammed the door and locked it. Then I practically flew upstairs to the sanctuary of my room. Fear followed me like a shadow.

Hurriedly slamming my bedroom door, I turned out the light, jumped into bed, and pulled the covers over my head. I heard a strange noise and strained my ears to hear above the pounding of my heart. The sound of footsteps coming up the stairs grew louder as they approached my door.

The turning of the doorknob and the squeaking of hinges announced that someone had entered my room. Suddenly the darkened room filled with light, which filtered through my heavy bed covers.

Unable to stand the suspense any longer, I decided to face the intruder. I pulled back the covers, and the room blazed into view as though a ball of fire was glowing in the midst. Brilliant rays of light dazzled me. Too blinded and frightened to look, a sense of reverence caused me to slip from my bed and onto the floor. A holy presence filled the room, and I began to cry and pray, "Help me, oh, Lord. I'm afraid. Help me, God!"

As I pleaded, a calmness spread over me and soothed my fears. With my head still bowed, I timidly opened my eyes. Looking down, I saw sandaled feet beneath a beautiful, flowing white garment that shimmered with radiant splendor. I reached out to touch them. They were real. Overwhelmed, I raised my eyes and looked into the face of Jesus.

I couldn't take my eyes off Him. He placed His left hand on my head, looked down at me, and smiled. My fears vanished as calmness and tranquility encompassed me.

Jesus pointed to a white Bible He held in His right hand. He said, "I want you to preach this," and moved His hands across the pages where the Bible was opened. I saw that the words were written in gold.

"But, Lord, I'm too young to preach," I said.

He smiled and answered, "Age doesn't matter. Time is short, and I am coming soon."

With those words, He vanished. I was left alone, kneeling by my bed in the darkness.

When my parents arrived home after a lengthy church service, they were pleasantly surprised to find me having my own church service.

Once again, God clearly confirmed His will for my life: I was to preach the gospel. However, several years would pass before I obeyed.

When I did finally yield to the Lord and start my preaching ministry, I used a white Bible. And I still carry one today.

Maybe the Lord will never speak to you as He spoke to me, but He speaks to all of us from His Word. He wants intimate fellowship with us, and He wants us to obey Him.

Some people wait, and they lose God's best because they live their entire lives waiting. Isaiah 55:7 says, "Let the wicked forsake his way. . .and let him return unto the Lord. . .for he will abundantly pardon."

Is Jesus knocking at your door? Let Him in, and watch your life be completely revolutionized.

Chapter Six

ONE SHALL BE TAKEN

"There's no way I'm going to go to Bible school,"
I determined as I walked down the path to the barn.
My parents had just given me all the reasons I should
go to Bible school in Seattle.

Seething, I backed the tractor out of the barn and
drove it onto the field. Soon I was plowing long furrows and watching the rich, brown soil separate and
fall to each side of the plowshare. Accompanied by a
steady increase of birds, I watched them dive into the
furrows and come up with long, juicy worms.

"I sure made their work easy for them!" I laughed.

My laughter faded as the voices of my parents' insistence rang in my ears: "Now that you've finished
high school, you really should attend Bible school."

I bet all preachers want their kids to go to Bible
school, I fumed and jerked the tractor around a big
stump. The only thing is, I'm not saved, and I don't
want to get involved with the kind of people that go
to Bible school.

My desire to preach had diminished. Because I found
it hard to be serious for long, I got distracted easily during church and rarely retained anything of the sermon.

I didn't want to be called a sissy by the other fellows so I avoided spending time at the altar. My greatest fear, however, was admitting to Mom and Dad that I had grown cold in my commitment.

The sunlight vanished when the shadows of dark clouds fell on the ground. Glancing at the sky, I noticed foreboding clouds gathering suddenly, as they often do in the plains states. I'd better get back to the house before a storm comes, I thought. In reflection, I said aloud, "You know, God would really have to do something drastic to convince me to go to Bible school."

The words had barely escaped my lips when the boom of a thunderclap almost shook me off the tractor seat. Regaining my balance, I quickly retracted the plowblade and was turning the tractor in the direction of the barn when a jagged streak of lightning flashed across the sky. One deadly finger reached down and struck my watch. The jolt I received literally caused my hair to stand on end. The peat moss seemed to vibrate for five hundred feet all around me.

When I finally caught my breath, I examined my watch. It was destroyed; but, to my amazement, I was still alive and unhurt. By the time I got back to the house, I had made a pact with God—I would go to Bible school.

As I drove into the barn, I decided that maybe the lightning had been a coincidence. So I added a conditional clause to my pact: "God, if You will arrange for the balance to be paid on my car, I will go."

I owed over three hundred dollars. If God could arrange the payoff that I knew neither my parents nor I could manage, it would serve to confirm that God had sent the lightning bolt.

Shortly after supper, Francis and Olga Ouverson, members of our church, dropped by. My parents called me into the living room, where they sat with satisfied smiles on their faces. Francis said, ''Ken, we felt God speak to us today. You need to go to Bible school, but you can't do it and make car payments, too. So we'll make the payments for you, and you'll have the car to use at school. That way we can be a part of the ministry we feel God has for you.''

I sat down as my knees buckled. Meekly, I muttered, ''Thanks, I do appreciate it.''

Knowing God had definitely spoken to me about going to Bible school, I wrestled again with my thoughts. God, visit me again. Speak to me. I soon found that God speaks in many ways.

On The Edge Of Death

While driving down a long stretch of Iowa road one day, I decided to force a confrontation with God. I pushed the gas pedal to the floor and roared down the gray ribbon of highway toward its never-ending horizon. If I die, then I will get God's attention. Then He will talk to me!

Stalks of corn went by in a blur as I sped to destruction. Sanity suddenly returned, and I thought, If I die, I'll go to hell. I can't go to hell. But I can't preach and do what I want to do, either.

I pulled off the road onto the shoulder edged by barbed wire fencing and realized I had been pulled back from the brink of eternity. I dropped my head onto the steering wheel and cried, ''God, why do You spare me?

Why do You want me?"

I shuddered to remember the close calls I had survived—not just from the recent lightning bolt but other catastrophes also.

The previous winter, Bob and I ran out of gas during a blizzard. While we waited for someone to come by, the wind whipped snow into drifts that threatened to bury us. Having been told never to leave the spot where you were stranded until rescue came, we stayed put. When the conditions were so bad we knew no one would come by, Bob and I realized we would freeze to death if we stayed any longer. The pelting snow and driving winds had drastically converted the familiar countryside into an alien world, and we didn't know which direction to go as we left the shelter of the car.

Walking and praying, we stumbled along hand-in-hand, blindly falling in snowdrifts, completely unaware of where we were. The bone-chilling, twenty-below-zero temperature was unbearable, and we could go no farther. At the point of collapsing, we stumbled providentially into the side of a house. We felt our way to the door, laughing and crying with relief as we were welcomed into warmth and light. I knew the Lord had heard our prayers and rescued us from sure death.

My life was miraculously spared another time. While driving down the road, I saw a tornado moving toward me at an incredible speed. Suddenly, my car was sucked up by the tremendous vacuum of the tornado. As I whirled around and around, I was horrified to find myself looking down on the tops of trees and telephone poles.

Just as suddenly, I was placed back down on the road, landing as gently as if I had been placed in the middle of feather ticking.

The tornado passed on, roaring out of sight, churning up the farmland a mile wide, and belching out digested debris. I looked at the trees with shafts of straw driven through them and knew that, once again, God had placed His arm of safety around me.

Humble Beginnings

In October, 1953, my parents drove with me to Seattle, where I was to attend Bethel Temple Bible School. My worldly goods consisted of a car, a Bible, a trumpet, a few clothes, and seventeen dollars; but I planned to make a good impression, especially on the girls.

The college was an extension ministry of Bethel Church. As I walked into that big, beautiful church, I spotted a pretty girl sitting in the choir. I whispered to my mother, "You see that blonde up there? I'm going to get to know her." Because of the looks this lovely singer kept sneaking at me, I felt I had a good chance.

Little did I realize the kind of impression I was making on her. Barbara turned to the girls beside her and said humorously, "That boy who just came in looks as though he came straight off the farm. He probably just scraped the manure off his shoes."

I suppose I *was* a comical sight in my double-breasted, red pin-striped suit that had been salvaged from a missions barrel. The pants were two inches above my ankles, and the jacket hung loosely on my lean frame. Although Barbara's first impression of me was not the best, I had determined to make her notice me.

After I was settled at the Bible school, Mom and Dad returned to Iowa, leaving me to find a job to support myself through school. But jobs were scarce, and my seventeen dollars soon ran out. Finally, another student and I moved into an apartment for a period of time. Together we split expenses, or you might say we split carrots. That was all we had to eat for several weeks—for breakfast, lunch, and dinner. We boiled, fryed, and cooked those carrots. When we received some pancake mix, we were thrilled. But we had only water to mix with it, and the pancakes tasted rather bland. At night I lay in bed dreaming of my favorite food: Mom's macaroni and raisins with fried bread. I was homesick.

Pride prevented my roommate and me from letting others know of our circumstances. Not eating properly caused me to become lethargic during classes, and I couldn't comprehend many things. To make matters worse, in spite of my many years of Sunday school and church, I had never paid much attention to spiritual truths. When I had my first class on the book of Revelation and we read the part where John spoke of opening the seals, I didn't know if we were studying church prophecy or talking about the zoo!

A few weeks before Christmas, I finally got a job as a carry-out boy in a grocery store for sixteen dollars a week. Soon I found a better paying job at a peanut butter factory working a four-to-twelve o'clock shift, which enabled me to continue going to school in the mornings. But the job was short-lived, and discouragement soon overwhelmed me.

The Voice Of Conscience

My desperate situation forced me to consider an alternative lifestyle, so I decided to enlist in the Air Force. At the recruiting station, I filled out the forms and was issued equipment. After waiting for some time, I was told to come back a few hours later to be sworn in because the officer had not yet arrived.

Back in the apartment I wrote a letter to my parents telling them I had joined the Air Force and was quitting Bible school. I felt grieved in my spirit because I knew how much joy my being there gave them. I thought, What's wrong with me anyhow? I'm not happy here, and I'm not happy when I think about leaving.

A still, small voice penetrated my subconscious. "You belong here. I want you to preach."

Suddenly afraid of what methods God might use to convince me this time, I drove quickly all the way back to the Air Force recruiting station. When I walked in, the sergeant greeted me, "Can I help you, boy?"

"Yes, sir. *I quit!*" I responded. "I just joined, but I quit!"

The officer looked sternly at me and said, "You can't quit if you're in."

I slapped the issued equipment down on his desk and said wildly, "I do quit! I can't go! I changed my mind. Here's the stuff that was issued to me."

He commanded me to sit down and went to the files to get my papers. As he pulled out my file and looked it over, I heard him muttering under his breath. There was a long, agonizing silence. He finally determined that I had not been officially sworn in.

Delighted that I was not officially in the Air Force, I jumped up and said, "Thanks, sir," and left before he could pressure me into a commitment.

My situation, however, had not changed, and I found myself asking the same question, How am I going to exist without a job? I felt relieved when one of the older students, Charlie Green, an Eskimo boy from Alaska, invited me to share his apartment over a Chinese laundry.

The apartment consisted of a bed, a refrigerator, and a hot plate, but it seemed like heaven. After much looking, I finally found a job in a hotel as a dishwasher. I moved up to janitor, busboy, waiter, and finally cook, which enabled me to help Charlie with half the expenses.

During this time, the Lord once again began to deal with me about committing my life totally to Him. But I tried to stay busy and not listen to my conscience.

When I went to church, I paid little attention to the message because of the turmoil it created—the demand of choosing between preaching and entertaining. I began to skip church services.

I couldn't get saved now, I convinced myself. My parents think I'm saved. What if they heard that I had repented? They would know I had been living a lie all this time.

I did enjoy helping others even though I wasn't born again. When I heard about the plight of one of the new Bible students, I decided to help him. Remembering my early days of discouragement, I paid his tuition for the quarter and bought him some groceries. I felt so good about it that I decided to buy him a much-needed coat. Reason told me that my doing good would help me find favor with God; thus, I quieted my conscience.

One of these days, I thought, I'll be through with this Bible school and will have pleased my parents. Then I can finally get into show business.

Standing On Shaky Ground

Charlie noticed I wasn't attending church so he started needling me about going with him. His constant hounding finally made me consent to go.

The evangelist who was speaking that night was well-known and said to be outstanding, so I felt he merited enough interest to go. He began his sermon with, "Make up your mind whether you're going to be good or bad. There are bad people in this world."

He pointed his long finger at me, but I knew no one had had a chance to tell him my name. "There are people who lie like the devil." Again he seemed to point right at me. I slid down in the pew.

"Furthermore," he stated, "one day one shall be taken, and one shall be left. Two shall be in a bed. One shall be taken, and one shall be left."

I gripped the seat until my knuckles turned white. "Charlie," I said, "You told them I moved in with you!"

The preacher continued, "When that happens, it's going to be a *great time!*"

The audience responded with a hearty, "Amen!"

Then he had the audacity to say, "It's going to be a *terrible time!*"

Again the response was, "Amen!"

I glanced around at their enraptured faces and thought, I wish they would make up their minds. I don't know if it's going to be good or bad.

Bits and pieces of some of Dad's sermons concerning the second coming of the Lord ran helter-skelter through my mind. I suddenly grew afraid. I *knew* I wasn't saved. The message brought vivid images to my mind of being left behind when Jesus comes back.

Immediately after the benediction, I hurried home and went to bed. I didn't want to have a discussion with Charlie. I just wanted to go to sleep and try to forget what I had heard that night. But sleep escaped me, and

I was still awake when Charlie arrived home. He came into the bedroom carrying his big Bible, one of those family-sized ones with a big tassel hanging out of it. He carried that Bible everywhere.

Charlie dressed for bed and got ready for his nightly prayer ritual. He knelt beside the bed and asked me, "Aren't you going to pray before you go to sleep?"

"No," I replied sullenly and turned over.

Praying out loud, Charlie began, "Dear God, that was a wonderful message tonight. One shall be taken, and one shall be left. I'm the one that's going, and Ken's the one that will be left."

I threw a pillow over my head and tried to block out his prayer. Finally, Charlie went to bed, and I soon dozed off to sleep. Around 2 a.m., I was literally shaken awake. The bed was bumping, and I heard the windows rattling. Dishes fell out of the cupboard and crashed to the floor. I opened my eyes, and watched a bottle of hair oil "walk" its way across the chest of drawers and crash to the floor.

Sitting upright in bed with fear choking my throat, I gasped, "Charlie, this is it! The Lord is coming!"

I reached over to shake Charlie and discovered that he was gone! I thought, Oh, no! This really is it! They've pulled it off! They've made it work! I am stranded! *Charlie's gone and I'm left!*

I shot out of the bed and flew across the undulating floor, throwing pillows, sheets, and blankets in every direction as I struggled to unwind them from my body. The words of Jim Downs, my Sunday school teacher, rushed through my mind: "Ken, you're going to keep on playing around with God, and one of these days Jesus will come and you'll be left behind."

52

I bumped into the door, ran into the front room, and staggered as the floor vibrated with each step I took. Crying and sobbing, I reached for the light cord that hung from the ceiling in the middle of the room. As I pulled the cord, I tripped across something on the floor and jerked the cord so hard it came out of the socket.

Light filled the room, and I realized I had fallen on Charlie, who had been sleeping on a folding cot in the middle of the living room. He sat sprawled on the floor, blinking in bewilderment. Relief flowed over me. He was not gone!

I shook him hard, screaming, "Charlie, I think the Lord has come."

He sat up, rubbed his bumped head, and stared sleepily at me. "What's the matter with you, Ken?"

"Charlie," I repeated, "the Lord has come!" My violent sobbing and screaming convinced Charlie that maybe He had come.

I grabbed his pajama collar in desperation and pleaded, "Pray for me, Charlie! I don't know how to pray. I think that the Lord has come. I believe now and want you to pray with me so I can find the Lord. Because if you're still here, He'll be back for a second load, and I want to be ready!"

Because I was somewhat confused about the way of salvation, Charlie explained it all to me. That night I preached my own sermon, gave my own altar call, and finally found the Lord.

The next day we discovered that the earthquake had affected one block and only rattled a few windows and bricks. It merited only a two-inch write-up in the newspaper. I called it "Ken Gaub's earthquake" because

I never forgot the jolt I received.

In Matthew's Gospel, chapter 24, Jesus states that He *will* return one day. Are you ready?

Being a "good person" is not enough. Paying your bills is not enough. Even being a good husband, wife, or parent is not enough. The Bible states that we can only be saved through faith in Jesus Christ. You might say, "I come from a religious background"—it still isn't enough.

I was a preacher's son, but I couldn't get to heaven because of my parents' experience. *I* had to meet Jesus Christ and accept Him into my life.

Each of us is responsible for our own life. 1 John 1:9 says, "If we confess our sins, he is faithful and just to forgive us our sins." Just walking into a church does not make us a Christian any more than walking into a fast food restaurant makes us a hamburger.

The Bible tells us in 2 Corinthians 5:17 that "if any man be in Christ, he is a new creature." Don't take chances. "One shall be taken, and one shall be left." If you don't know Him, accept Him now.

Chapter Seven

WHEELER DEALER

How am I going to stay in school if I can't find a job? I wondered as I searched the "Help Wanted" ads in the classified section of the Seattle newspaper.

Charlie, my roommate in Bethel Bible School, had graduated and moved back to Alaska. The expenses of the apartment we had shared became too great for my meager income alone. Gathering my few belongings together, I moved out. Thankfully, I did still have my car, which became my home. I ate, slept, and did my homework assignments in my car. More than once I went to class with a "crick" in my neck from a restless night sleeping cramped up on the front seat.

I found occasional odd jobs that kept me from starving, but I needed to find stable employment. Jobs in Seattle at that time, however, were scarce.

"I'll just have to make my own job," I declared.

The ability to devise ways of making money had always come easy to me. From the first strawberries I picked at nine years of age earning ten cents a basket, I have always enjoyed creating various means of generating funds. Money had been a precious commodity as I was growing up, and my mother scolded me for spending too much time on things that interfered with my schoolwork. "Who wants to sit in school all day and look out the window when there is work to be done?" I asked her. "There's money to be made out there."

I even got my mother involved in one of my money-making efforts. She agreed to make popcorn and bag it for a nickel a bag. I then approached my sister Shirley and asked, "Sis, how would you like to make a nickel on every bag of popcorn you sell for me?"

"Okay," she jumped at the opportunity, "how will I do that?"

"Easy," I explained with the suave assurance of a salesman. "I'll provide the popcorn, and you just sell it for twenty cents a bag. Then you keep five cents from each sale for yourself."

"Sounds good to me," she agreed.

After loading the bags of popcorn into a little red wagon, she went up and down the streets of our community selling all the popcorn Mom could pop. For each bag sold, I paid my mother and my sister each five cents. I made ten cents profit and did nothing.

When summer came with its harvest of pumpkins and watermelons, I used the same gimmick. My sister, however, finally realized that *she* was doing all the work and *I* was making all the money.

Gainful Employment

My financial needs in Bible school were much more urgent than those of my childhood. I didn't need nickels and dimes for candy and toys—I needed dollars to survive.

Automobiles had always held a fascination for me. Some of the most enjoyable hours of my mid-teen years were spent tinkering, tuning, and testing my own car or those of my friends. Owning a car was important to me because I realized how it impressed the girls. I even painted "Air Conditioning" on the side of the hood. On a hot day, I'd roll the windows up and drive around trying to look "cool," all the time sweltering in the heat. One of my mechanical innovations was a left-handed gear shift that enabled me to put my arm around a girl while I drove.

As I thought about my ability with cars, a money-making idea began to develop. I told a friend, "I'm going to create a job somewhere."

He scoffed, "There's no jobs in Seattle."

"Well then," I said, "I'll make one, and I'll make it work, too!"

The idea of using my mechanical ability and my passion for cars began to take root. Soon I had my plan of operation and walked to the office of a nearby used car lot to talk to the owner.

"I want to work for you," I said to the owner. Before he could respond, I continued, "I'll make my own job. I'll work one week for nothing. If you like what I do, I want the right to set my own wages and my own hours when I come in the following Saturday. If you don't like what I do, then just wave me goodbye. We'll shake hands, you'll have the money I have made for you, and I'll leave without a penny. I guarantee I'll increase your business."

"Well, young man, that sounds like a pretty bold claim. Just what kind of service do you propose to offer me?" he asked with a look of disbelief.

"I'm going to clean your cars," I announced as if it had never been thought of before.

"Naw!" he waved away the suggestion. "We've got guys cleaning up cars already."

Finally, I convinced him to give me a try. After selecting a nice-looking car from the lot, I parked it out of view of the other employees. I then proceeded to refurbish the car from bumper to bumper.

Before washing and waxing the exterior, I touched up all the nicks and scratches. I painted the floor mats, tires, and even inside the trunk with black paint to give them a fresher appearance. I cleaned every inch of the interior, including ash trays and the glove compartment. The car took on a new appearance. Even the engine was steamed until there wasn't any sign of previous use. I stood back to admire my work. To me, it looked brand-spanking new.

Then I laid my hands on the car hood and began to pray, "Lord, I believe You gave me this idea. I need You to sell this car because I have to eat."

When I walked into the dealer's office the next day, he told me the car had been sold. I cleaned three more cars, not sparing a single detail in their cleaning. As I finished, I prayed over each of them. By Friday all three cars were gone, and none of the others on the lot had been sold.

On Saturday, the dealer called me into his office. He was convinced that I had lived up to my promise and thrust out his hand to shake on the deal I had previously offered.

"Okay, you got the job. You have made an impression. What's your price?"

Before he could change his mind, I proceeded, "I

want one hundred dollars a car. I'll work my own hours and supply the materials for the clean up. If I have someone help me, I'll pay them. All you have to do is pay me one hundred dollars for each car."

He whistled. "That's a bit stiff, young fellow," he said. After convincing him that the profit from the cars I cleaned would more than offset my fee, he finally agreed.

I hired boys from school to clean the cars and paid them fifty dollars for each car they reconditioned. God sent buyers for the cars we cleaned, and we prospered as money rolled in.

The Joy Of Sharing

God was the source of my prosperity, and I wanted to show my gratitude by sharing my blessings. I especially enjoyed giving a hundred-dollar bill in the offering plate of a small church. The surprised response of a treasurer as he or she counted the Sunday school offering was very amusing.

I liked walking up to a discouraged preacher and saying, "Here, I want to give you something."

"Why that's a hundred-dollar bill!" some would say in disbelief, wondering if I had made a mistake.

"Oh, you're kidding! Let me see it! Why it *is,* isn't it?" I teased.

Many acknowledged that it was an answer to prayer. It gave me a great sense of satisfaction to know that God, in meeting my financial needs, was also using me to help others.

The Bible says, "Give and it shall be given unto you" (Luke 6:38). I have found that you can't outgive God.

The more generous you are, the more blessings will come back to you. Philippians 4:19 reads, "My God shall supply all your need according to his riches in glory by Christ Jesus." Over the last few years I have given something away every day. Sometimes I have bought someone lunch—sometimes just a cup of coffee.

Whatever we have in us is what comes out. If we have faith, an encouraging spirit, a positive attitude, answers, love, joy, happiness, etc., we will radiate this. On the other hand, if we are full of fear, bad attitudes, hatred, envy, wrath, strife, etc., our lives will reflect these negative feelings.

An old story says that when the Berlin Wall was being built, the Russians loaded a truck with rotten garbage, sewage, etc. They then proceeded to back up to the wall and dump it onto the Western side. The Western people had to clean up this awful mess. Then *they* got a truck, loaded it up, and dumped it on the Russian side. However, their truck was filled with canned food and clothes for boys and girls. In the middle of their load, they placed a sign written in German. The sign simply read, *"Each One Gives What He Has."*

Chapter Eight

BARBARA

Barbara—I couldn't get her out of my mind. From my first day on Bethel Bible School campus, when I spotted her singing in the church choir, I was determined to win her affections. Yet, I never could summon the courage to act upon my feelings. Several months passed before I became brave enough to ask her out.

My own backslidden spiritual condition was the principal reason I waited so long to ask Barbara out. She was a dedicated Christian, and the respect and admiration I held for her greatly enhanced my infatuation. In my mind, I had placed her on a high pedestal.

Following my total rededication to Christ, I began to get my life in order once and for all. I hoped that Barbara would see the change, knowing that any fellow fortunate enough to date her would have to be both a Christian and a gentleman.

After discovering through a mutual friend that Barbara thought I had a "magnetic personality," I determined to "sweep her off her feet."

One Saturday evening, I saw her at the youth service at Bethel Church. With all the "magnetism and personality" I could muster, I casually but confidently walked up to Barbara and asked, "Hey, do you have a ride?"

She hesitated, then cooly replied, "Yes, I have a ride."

Needless to say, that dealt my ego a devastating blow. I replied, "Okay, see you later," and sauntered away to join my other friends. Little did I know that her ride was with another girl. She just wanted me to think she had a date in order to hide her interest in me. Of course, her scheme worked, and I resolved more than ever to get a date with her.

The next time I asked Barbara for a date, I was less brash, and she accepted my invitation. From the beginning, I believed that she was to be my wife. However, several weeks passed before I could convince Barbara.

I soon found I could tell her things I had never been able to tell anyone else. As I shared with Barbara my dream of being like Oral Roberts, she understood and encouraged me to believe God had a special plan for my life. Her calmness was a balance for my impulsive nature.

For her eighteenth birthday in July, I managed to save enough money for a diamond ring. We set the date for the following September.

Just one hour before the wedding ceremony, I was up to my ears in grease trying to replace a piston in the car so we could leave on our honeymoon. Nothing seemed to be going right. In a moment of frustration, I told my best man, "What am I doing here? Why do I want to get married? Let's take off and run away." (I'm glad Barbara had the keys to the car!)

My frustration and apprehension disappeared the moment I saw Barbara in the chapel. Dressed in a white wool dress with a matching jacket and a little feather hat that emphasized her golden hair and large blue eyes, she looked beautiful.

We exchanged wedding vows, and the pastor pronounced us "man and wife." I knew I had made the right choice. Our wedding date of September 17, 1954, was the beginning of a new life for me. Barb not only became my marriage partner but also my best friend.

"Barb," I told her, "I want to be a different sort of preacher than what they teach in Bible school. This is all form, not reality. We're learning principles, not practicing faith. Faith works. I've seen it in my dad's life. But I think it's time to put into practice what I've learned."

One night in January, I was walking home from work and saw a phone number written on a door of a closed-up church. I copied the number and hurried home to tell Barbara. "Honey, let's see if we can rent this place. I want to do something for God. It's not enough to *learn* to be a preacher; I want to *practice* it."

Quickly, we got on the phone and discovered that the place had been closed for three years and seated sixty-five people. Twenty-six dollars still remained in the church treasury. The people were glad to rent it and even forwarded the offering, which we used to fix the building.

It took three weeks of cleaning and painting to get the place ready. Finally, we put up the sign that read, "Faith Tabernacle," and listed service times for Sunday morning, Sunday evening, and Monday and Friday evenings.

Soon people at Bethel Church asked, "Why haven't you been in church lately?"

Grinning from ear to ear, I said, "Hey, we've started our own church."

But even the *Faith Tabernacle* wasn't fulfilling enough. Anxious to be in full-time Christian service, I looked forward to graduation. As I spent time in prayer and fasting, a burden was growing within me for a particular group of people. I felt I knew where God was leading me.

Knowing we could soon be leaving for an area almost three thousand miles away, I made arrangements to leave Faith Tabernacle in the capable hands of a good brother.

Chapter Nine

THE PROMISED LAND

"We're going to Kentucky," I confidently told Barbara. "I know that's where God wants me."

"Kentucky! Why Kentucky?" she asked.

"Barbara, God has been speaking to me about people in Kentucky for several months now. Dad has always talked about the mission work he once did in Kentucky, and it must be important to God because I can't get the place off my mind. I *know* that must be where God wants us to go after graduation."

A vision of beautiful Kentucky stayed before me the remaining school days like the elusive carrot before the horse. I knew nothing about Kentucky except what I had seen illustrated in books. The vague descriptions I had from Dad of its mountains, valleys, creeks, and "hollers" filled my vision and drew me like a magnet. Anxious to fulfill my call, I prayed fervently for the people of Kentucky, claiming their souls for the Lord.

Graduation day, May 31, 1955, marked the beginning of our faith venture. Barb and I loaded the 1949 Nash with everything we possessed and set out on a three-thousand mile journey to Kentucky.

The thought of leaving behind everything familiar

made Barbara apprehensive. She grabbed my hand and said, "Ken, let's pray before we leave Seattle. I have an idea. If the Lord really wants us to stay and preach in Kentucky, He can prove it to us. Let's ask God to let us end our trip with exactly the same amount of money that we have now."

I agreed that it was a good idea. We prayed and then counted every cent we had between us. It would have to be a miracle just to *make* it to Kentucky with only twenty-one dollars. But we had big faith, and we were young and confident.

Our plan was simple: we would evangelize our way across the United States to Kentucky. We first stopped in Ellensburg, Washington, where my parents pastored. My mind teemed with visions of overwhelming success as a novice preacher. Fired with enthusiasm, I told Barbara, "I know that when I preach tonight the church is going to be packed, and the people are going to be swayed by the power of God like trees in the wind."

But either my preaching still lacked a lot of polish or the people had worked hard that day. They did sway as they nodded off to sleep. Undaunted, and with Barb's encouragement and some more practice sessions under my belt, I met with greater success during the next six weeks of cross-country evangelism.

We finally arrived at the Kentucky border and made our way across Pine Mountain. The town of Hazard lay tucked away in a narrow valley. Glancing up and down the streets of the town, we felt as though we had arrived in a foreign country. Mountains rose in every direction. Worn clapboard buildings stood on one side of the street, which ran parallel with a gurgling, rushing stream of water. Driving down Main Street, we noticed ladies in calico bonnets and homespun dresses. Men sat clustered in groups in front of a white, wooden courthouse chewing tobacco and passing the time of day.

As we pulled up to a parking place in town, Barbara looked around the quaint town and said, "We'd better count our money and make sure this is God's will!"

We had received offerings from churches where we had preached, and we had spent money for food and gas. We had no idea how much was left. I dumped all the change into Barb's lap and pulled the bills out of my billfold. After counting the bills, we breathlessly started a countdown on the change. It totaled exactly *twenty-one dollars!*

"Well, this is it," I said. " Let's find a place to live."

After purchasing a local paper, we looked at the available housing. Most places were too high, and we began to feel desperate. Finally we located two inexpensive rooms located in the back portion of a house. We had to share a bath with the landlady and several other boarders; but considering it was only ten dollars a week, it seemed like a bargain.

I was anxious to get out and meet with people. We soon discovered Kentucky mountain folks were friendlier and more appreciative than those we had been used to. Barb and I could see their hunger for the Word of God, and we fell in love with them.

We invited them to our revivals, which were held on porches, in the streets, and up the hollers under a grove of trees. People came from everywhere around Hazard. Many walked for miles to attend the meetings, which provided a social outlet for the mountain people.

The farther back in the mountains we visited, the less we saw of worldly wealth. Most of the homes were shacks, and many were built of logs with mud serving as a filler. We rarely saw running water or electricity. When winter snows came, the people suffered the hardships of being ill-fed and ill-clothed. But the summer months brought them an abundance of garden crops. I grew to love their main dishes of chicken, beans, potatoes, and cornbread, but I couldn't handle their traditional dish of fatback.

Sin and superstition bound our new-found friends. Few churches preached the full truth of the Bible. Scriptures were taken out of context, and doctrines such as snake-handling, fire-handling, live coal-handling, drinking deadly poison, and free love were being practiced.

We realized that the home missions project we had undertaken was not going to be easy. We were supported by various churches we had visited on the way to Kentucky and by our home church in Seattle. They also sent clothes and food for the needy. Once I received over two hundred pairs of shoes to give away. I had never seen so many excited people.

Grieved by the sorrows and needs of the poor mountain folk, I longed to hear them laugh and see them forget their troubles. I tried, but they were extremely financially pressed.

Because I wanted to reach every home possible, I spent hours visiting up and down the creeks and hollers.

One day, I passed an old mountain man rocking on his porch, so I stepped up and explained that I was the preacher in those parts and that we were starting a church. I wanted to talk to him about his soul.

He chomped down on his tobacco, leaned over, and spit off the porch, barely missing me. Then he looked me right in the eye and said, "I killed two men, and I'm a-fixing to get another."

I gulped and said, "God loves you, sir, and sent His Son to die for those sins you committed. Just accept Him as your Savior."

Looking me up and down, he glared at me. "Does it say in the Bible if a person has two coats, he's supposed to give one away?"

"Yes, sir," I replied, unsure of what he was getting at. "It says something like that."

"Well, son, do you have two shirts?" he asked, thrusting his hands under his suspenders.

"Yes, sir."

"Well, then," he said, reaching over and feeling the texture of my shirt between his fingers, "I'm a-asking you for the one you have on."

I did not expect this practical application of the gospel, but I pulled off my shirt and gave it to him. Then muttering an excuse, I said, "I guess I need to be getting on back home. My wife is expecting me soon," I left quickly, feeling I'd better get away before he asked for my pants, too.

One day as I prepared to do more visiting, the Lord spoke to me. "I want you to go back and visit the old man to whom you gave your shirt."

"Please, Lord, no," I pleaded.

But I knew better than to argue with the Lord. I wasn't cut out to be a Jonah. When I arrived back at the old log cabin, the mountain man was sitting in the same spot on the porch, rocking away and wearing my shirt.

He stared at me. Growing apprehensive, I prayed silently, "Are you sure, Lord, that I was supposed to come back here?"

This time when I told him about God's plan of salvation, he listened without interruption. Before long, he broke down and cried, and I led him in a sinner's prayer. When he began to take off my shirt to return it, I knew he was really saved. I let him keep the shirt. It had been worth it.

Any time we disobey and do not stay in God's will, we can cause others to be destroyed or lost forever. I once felt led to witness to a man at a gas station but didn't. After buying my gas, I drove down the road for about an hour. I felt so bad that I had to turn around and go back.

When I drove in, the man said, "Weren't you here a couple of hours ago?"

"Yes, I was," I said, "but I turned around."

He said, "I thought you were headed in the other direction."

I said, "I was, but I turned around." While he filled my tank, I said, "Sir, the reason I came back was to talk to you about eternity. Do you know Jesus Christ as your Savior?" Although I witnessed to him, he did not accept the Lord at that moment. But I felt I had obeyed the Lord.

Two weeks later, I drove through the same area, and I stopped again. Another man waited on me. I asked if the first man was there. "That was my father-in-law," he said, "and he was killed in a car wreck last week."

I don't know if he found the Lord before he died, but I do know that I had shown him the way to salvation. If he had time to call on God, he's in heaven right now.

Obedience is important. We never know when a person will enter eternity, and that's why the Bible tells us to be ready to witness "in season" and "out of season" (2 Timothy 4:2). Whether you are "in" or "out," keep alert and be willing to obey the Lord. He will direct you to the lost sheep of this world, and you can make a difference.

Chapter Ten

LIVING BY FAITH

"God, why don't you help a fellow sometimes?" I complained, too discouraged to get up from where I lay.

Never having built anything before, I had bought some new lumber and twenty-five pounds of crooked nails for fifty cents. Getting those nails back into shape stretched my sanctification all out of shape. I had to work with a broken hammer, a crooked saw, and an eleven-inch ruler. After finishing the twenty new church pews to use in the old rental house, I sat down with a sigh of relief. As I leaned back, the improperly built seat tilted backward. Over I went, knocking down the remaining pews as though they were dominoes.

I lay amid the unsightly pews and prayed, "Please God, help me. I don't know how to do this."

Getting up, I examined the benches. They were eighteen feet long and taller than they were wide. The legs narrowed toward the middle. I saw the problem and remodeled them, praying the whole time. After testing each pew by rocking back and forth, I decided it would take a bulldozer to push them over. But to make doubly sure, I nailed them to the floor.

Some of our converts helped with painting and repairing the leaky roof, and Barbara made curtains for the windows. We spent less than one hundred dollars converting the old house into a church building. It was now ready for Sunday services.

At this early stage of my ministry, my preaching was like a machine gun. I shot out words in rapid-fire succession, hardly pausing as word upon word came to my mind. I was afraid I might lose my "anointing" if I swallowed. The people, however, were patient and responded to my ministry in spite of my inexperience.

Although our little church started with only twelve people, we quickly grew to seventy-five. Within a short time, three hundred were attending.

Our meetings grew, and we rejoiced to see children come to accept Jesus as their Savior. Many of these children did not go to school. Truant officers couldn't locate families far back in the "hollers."

Seeing a need for special ministry to the children, we began a Vacation Bible School. Within three weeks, approximately twenty-five hundred school-age children were attending. Hundreds of them gave their hearts to the Lord.

The children we worked with in Vacation Bible School came to our Sunday school, also. They were ragged but happy to know that we cared about them. One Sunday morning a twelve-year-old girl came leading her two small sisters and carrying her eighteen-month-old brother. She had walked barefoot two and one-half miles through two inches of snow to get there. When she arrived, Barb and I rubbed her black and blue feet to bring back the circulation and then gave her a pair of shoes and socks. Her big smile and faithful attendance was all the reward we needed. In cold, heat, or snow, she came.

Spiders And Snakes

We walked to our church through a tangled path that ran down through the woods and across a portion of railroad track. One evening a copperhead struck at the accordion case I was carrying for Barb. Needless to say, we arrived at the service a little sooner than normal. The experience kept us prayed up going to and from church.

After several weeks, I grew used to the walk and wasn't as concerned about watching my step. When we reached the railroad track one day, I heard a rattle. Quickly, I stopped and looked around. Not seeing anything, I started forward again.

Ssss! The warning rattle of a snake sounded close by. I was puzzled. Then I felt a crawly sensation on my leg. I slowly pulled up my pant leg and saw the body of a large rattler winding himself around my leg. My foot was on his head. Unable to move his head, he had begun his warning rattle.

For a moment I froze! I didn't dare move my foot! Then, with all my strength, I began grinding his head into the ground with my foot and praying as fast as I could. He soon loosened his grip and fell loosely coiled around my ankle. "It sure would be easy to have a snake-handling meeting around here," I said, faking calmness.

Even the churchhouse wasn't safe from intruding snakes. A copperhead attended services one busy evening and coiled up on the platform to stare at me. He slithered away before anyone could decide what to do. Attempting to maintain my composure, I went back to preaching.

A few nights later, two spiders larger than silver dollars attended the service. The people seated close by jumped up on the pews. (I was glad I had nailed the seats to the floor.) In the middle of my sermon, I stopped, grabbed the broom, and tried to kill the spiders. They kept a leap ahead and managed to escape.

I said, "After all, even Moses had to deal with serpents and scorpions."

Barb retorted, "You just attract unusual sorts."

Special Delivery

Besides snakes and spiders, we faced many other challenges, including raising financial support.

Our average offering brought about one dollar. Once we received the tremendous sum of $2.00. Barb and I lived on what was given to us and the money our supporting churches sent from time to time. Our faith was tested continually.

At one point, all we had was salt, pepper, and a little dab of corn flakes left to eat. We also had a bill for ten dollars due that very day. As we knelt to thank God for His provision, I told Barb, "I believe the Lord has heard our prayers. He has always answered on time. I'm going to the post office to get our mail because I feel there's going to be a letter with money in it."

At the post office, I walked up to the window, smiled at the postmaster, and said, "I'll take my mail."

Still sorting the mail, he glanced up and replied, "There's no mail for you today."

I thrust my hands into empty pockets and returned to the car. As I opened the door and started to get in, the thought struck me, Wait a minute! I just asked God to have mail for me, and I'm going back in to get it.

Back at the General Delivery window, I cleared my throat to get the postmaster's attention and said, "I'll take my mail, please!" I thrust out my hand to receive it.

He looked up at me with a bewildered expression. "*Ain't* no mail here for you. You just checked a few minutes ago."

I insisted, "I know, but there's a letter now."

"Nope!" he said. "Ain't been nary a truck come in. Can't be no letter."

Seeing the determination on my face, he gave in. "Okay, I'll check again. Though won't do no good. There ain't no mail for you. I oughta know. I handle all the mail that comes in here."

I repeated, "I know, but there *is* a letter for me in there now."

He reached back into the slot marked "G" and, with a stunned look on his face, pulled out a letter and stared at it. He shook his head and handed it to me. It was from Jim Cahill, Seattle, Washington. Pointing at the mark stamped just ten hours before, the postmaster said in amazement, "This can't be! It takes three, sometimes four *days* for a letter to come from that far away. How did it get here in ten hours? How did it get in this box?"

"God did it!" I replied. "I don't think that letter was there when I first came in, but I needed it. When I prayed, faith entered my heart; and I told the Lord, 'I'm going back in there and get it.' Then God reached down into the mail plane and, quicker than air mail, flipped the letter down into the box just for me."

"Imagine that," the postmaster said, still puzzled. "Hey, look at that!" Still staring at the letter, he pointed at the stamp. "That letter hasn't even got a regular general delivery stamp on it like we stamp every letter that comes through our office. You must be right!" he remarked with a note of wonder in his voice.

Waving the letter triumphantly in the air, I raced home to Barbara with the letter from heaven that held a check—a check that more than met our financial needs.

We received money miraculously, though not as dramatically, on numerous other occasions. People were praying for our needs, and the money always arrived from anonymous sources.

Supernatural Service

We prayed continually for money to meet our needs so we could maintain our visitation program around Hazard. One day I was left with one dollar to purchase gas.

During my prayer time, I told the Lord, "I'm doing this for you and your people. Here I am without gas again, and my wife and I need to get to the service tonight. All we have is one dollar to last until your next miracle."

"What can I do for you?" the attendant asked as Barb and I pulled up to the pump of the local gas station. With as much pride as if I were getting a fillup, I said, "Give me a dollar's worth."

After five minutes had passed, Barb asked, "Isn't he taking a long time just to put in a dollar's worth?"

Turning to look out the open window to where the attendant was pumping gas, I saw him shaking his head and mumbling, "Man, it's taking a long time for this gas to go in."

Looking at my gas gauge, I saw the needle moving over toward "Full." "I hope he remembers that I told him just one dollar's worth," I said to Barb.

I yelled back, "Hey, I just want a dollar's worth!"

"Yeah, I know," he replied. He pointed to the pump gauge, which registered $.25. "Something's wrong. This stuff sure is going in slow."

Finally, he put away the hose and came to collect my dollar. When I drove away, my tank was full.

By now our car had accumulated an abundance of miles traveling through the hills of Kentucky, and we needed a new one. As I was on the way to a meeting one day, the car conked out. I pushed it over to the side of the road and worked on it for over an hour.

Disgusted, I looked at it and put down my tools. "Lord," I said, "I can't do anything else with this car. Maybe You can. The Bible says to ask anything in Your name and You'll do it. Now I'm asking."

Reaching out and putting one hand on the engine, I lifted the other hand in the air and began praying out loud. I failed to hear the police officer pull up as I intently prayed, "Lord, please look down and fix the engine. I can't do it, and I need Your help."

The policeman waited until I finished and then tapped me on the shoulder. When I turned to see who was there, he looked at me and said, "What in the world are you doing?"

I said matter-of-factly, "I'm praying for my car."

"Oh, what's wrong with it?" he asked.

I shrugged and wiped the tears off my cheeks. "I don't know. That's why I'm praying for it."

Pushing aside his helmet, he scratched his head. "You think it'll start now?"

"Yes," I nodded, "God fixed it. I'll get in, and it will run."

He laughed, "Before you get too excited, you'd better get in and try it. If it doesn't work, I'll call somebody."

"Don't worry," I replied as I cleaned up my hands and slammed the hood. "When I pray, it works."

As I got into the car, the devil told me, "You're making a big fool of yourself! You'll *never* win that man to God. This is not going to be a testimony. He'll laugh at you."

Refusing to let those words sink into my brain, I turned the key. The engine started immediately. I looked up into the face of the policeman as if God fixed cars everyday.

His face had turned pale, and tears formed in his eyes. "Man, I've seen everything!"

I told him that this was just the beginning of what God could do. After I told him about Jesus, he drove off on his motorcycle a different man.

Growing In Faith

Not only was our church growing, but our family was expanding as well. Nathan Lee was born squalling into the world at 2:35 a.m. on November 11, 1955. "Twenty-five inches! That is the longest baby ever born in this area!" the doctor said after measuring him twice to make sure. Two weeks later we proudly carried

Nathan to Sunday school.

When our car finally wore out, someone gave us another one. At Christmas we loaded it with gifts for some of our needy church members. We had fun sneaking up to their doors, knocking, and then hiding before the recipients could see who had left the packages. The work was fun, but demanding, and took its toll on us.

Barb and I both became sick with mountain fever from drinking water back in the hollers. I tried to help Barb by taking turns getting up with Nathan at night. The previous day he had begun to whine and refused to nurse. He had caught the fever from Barbara.

When I got up to check on him during the night, I discovered he was cold. As I spoke to him, I noticed his legs and arms were stiff. I grabbed him and shook him, but he wouldn't open his eyes. Trying to decide whether or not to awaken Barbara, I grew frightened. I held our baby close and reached out desperately to God: "Lord, if you take our baby, I'll never preach another sermon. I couldn't have faith. Please heal him."

Not only did God heal Nathan, but He healed all of us. By the next morning, we were all back to normal—happy and healthy.

Life responds to our outlook. If we speak success, it will uplift us and help us succeed. If we speak fear and failure, it will increase its grip upon us and hold us in bondage. I have always tried to speak positively, even when I faced problems that seemed impossible. When we say we are going to fail, we are saying that God is not big enough to solve the problem. Paul said in Philippians 4:13, "I can do all things through Christ who strengtheneth me." That includes succeeding. *I can succeed through Christ who strengthens me.*

Chapter Eleven

MOVING HIGHER

Visiting the sick was one of my regular activities. I had been ministering to a year-old baby who had been admitted to the local hospital. The father, however, didn't believe in prayer and grew angry whenever his wife mentioned church, so I had to pray for the baby in secret. The mother usually met me and took me to the baby's hospital room when the father wasn't there. If I saw the father leaving, I knew I could stop to pray.

One particular day, my shoes were making a tapping sound that seemed more noticeable in the unusually quiet hallway outside the baby's room. No one was around, so I peeked into the baby's room. I crept over to the crib where the baby lay covered with a sheet. Reaching out my hand, I softly touched the sheet covering the baby so as not to awaken him. "Lord," I prayed, "raise up this baby for Your glory."

Noticing that the baby had started squirming, I decided to go before it cried and attracted attention. Just as I turned to leave, I saw that the doorway was blocked by the large frame of the father, who stood glaring at me. He glanced over at the bed and, seeing the sheet moving, cried, "Oh, God!"

He stood there screaming while I tried to think of something to say. By now the commotion had attracted the attention of the nurse. "Please, sir," she said. "Calm down. This is a hospital. I realize this is hard on you."

The father kept on crying and pointing to the baby. Then the nurse looked at the crib, and she screamed. All the color faded from her face as she backed out the door and ran down the corridor. I didn't know what to do.

Finally, the father went over and picked up the child. I thought, This baby must be dying. Not wanting to cause any family problems, I quietly left.

When the hospital called to say that the parents had asked me to return, I assumed the baby had died—either that or I was going to be reprimanded for intruding. Not knowing what to expect, I was flabbergasted when the smiling father rushed up and threw his arms around me. "Preacher, I want to tell you I changed my mind about that religious stuff. I believe now!" He began weeping again and couldn't talk.

"What's going on?" I asked.

The mother finally spoke up. "Didn't you know that our baby died two hours before you came?"

"What? No, I didn't."

"What happened, preacher?" the father asked.

"Well, I felt I had to pray for that baby. I didn't know he was dead. I just asked God to raise him up for His glory."

Soon afterward, this man was led to salvation, and most of his relatives and other acquaintances also turned to God. The baby boy grew up, got married, and is alive today as a living testimony of God's healing power.

The Hazardous Deluge

God often delivered us from impending doom by speaking directly to my heart, as He did when a flood threatened our home.

"Water, water everywhere and not a drop to drink." Worry swirled about my mind like the flood waters rushing past me. After purchasing a house trailer, Barb and I had parked it in a trailer village on the banks of the river that ran through Hazard. The murky waters were rising steadily from the heavy rains that had descended daily. A growing concern swept through the village as the waters climbed at the rate of a foot or so a night.

I prayed, "God, what should I do? I don't want to panic, but I am thinking about my wife and baby and everything we own. I don't want to lose them."

A group of neighbors congregated outside, and I went out to join them. Someone commented, "We don't have to worry." Pointing to a low depression in the street, he said, "That dip out there fills with water in every rain, but then it goes down. We're high enough to be safe."

But the Lord spoke to me, "Move out quickly!"

I told the group, "I'm going to move out. God told me to move."

I hitched our jeep to the trailer and unhooked all the phone and electrical wires. Several of the people who had been living along the bank of the river for years stood and remarked, "He's the panicky sort, ain't he?"

Then one of the men said seriously, "I believe this man. If he thinks God told him to get out, I think maybe He wants me to move out, too."

I pulled my trailer to a high hill where the Spirit had impressed me to go. Then I came back to help the other man out.

The river rose at an alarming rate that evening. The water in the dip never went down. Soon the eighteen-foot telephone pole that had stood beside our trailer was completely covered with violently swirling muddy water. Homes and trailers floated downstream, bobbing along in an unorderly fashion.

Many lives were lost in the flood, but we were safe and warm in our trailer high upon the hill. *Life Magazine*, January, 1957, carried pictures of the terrible destruction in Hazard.

A Timely Furlough

As a result of our obedience during the flood, our visitation program was more readily received. They often said, "God speaks to him." Determined to give the people the best I could, I visited and handed out supplies sent to relieve the flood victims. Barbara and I were already exhausted from our normal routines.

One evening, I felt I could make it no longer. After a full day of visitation, I came in and fell across the bed. My left side had been aching, and my arms throbbed with pain. As my heart began jerking irregularly in my chest, I cried aloud. Barbara heard my moan and ran into the room. Taking one look at me, she fell to her knees. She had no time to call a doctor, but her prayer reached heaven. Suddenly, I was free from pain.

We knew then that we needed a vacation from the strenuous work. Barbara had lost forty pounds, and I had lost seventeen. We decided to visit my folks back in Washington. We wrote ahead for speaking engagements at the churches that supported us and planned to give them a report of our missions work in the Kentucky mountains.

The day of our departure was Friday the thirteenth, and the superstitious folks around us begged us to wait until the next day. Laughing, we drove away to prove that Satan has no power over the children of God.

Because we had no money for motels, we drove straight through from Kentucky to Iowa on the first leg of our journey. The temperature was below zero, and the car heater worked only part of the time. Driving through the bitter cold with blankets wrapped around us, we were concerned for Nathan. After ministering in only a few churches, we decided to head straight for Washington.

By the time we reached Colorado, I was concerned about our financial situation and pulled into a grocery store parking lot so we could discuss our problem. I told Barbara, "Honey, we've got only twenty cents left and over eleven hundred miles to our next stop. What are we going to do?"

She said, "We do what we preach. We believe the Lord and pray."

Ashamed that I had doubted, I dropped my head, and Barb and I asked the Lord to send help. Then I drove in faith to a service station and sat there wondering just what step to take next. In my rearview mirror, I noticed another car pull in behind us. A lady got out, came over, and peeked in my window. "Are you folks on vacation?" she asked.

"No," I replied. "We're on our way to Idaho. We do

gospel work."

Very excitedly, she said, "I saw you parked back by the grocery store with your heads bowed. I told my husband that I believed you were Christians and that you were praying for financial assistance. I want to help you."

Reaching in the window, she placed twenty-five dollars in my hand. I stared at it, not knowing whether to laugh or cry. I said, "Lady, I will never forget this. Thank you so much."

Barbara echoed my sentiments and our eyes filled with tears.

"Don't thank me, thank the Lord," she said and pulled away. We sat there still staring at the miracle in our hands.

By the time we reached the state of Washington, the car was making strange noises. From my experience with cars, I knew the rods were going out. However, we were confident that God was with us and would keep the car operating until we reached my parents' home in Ellenburg. When we pulled into the driveway, the engine quit before I could even turn off the ignition switch.

Although they were thrilled to see us again, my parents were shocked at how thin we both were and the poor condition of our clothes. Mom enjoyed "fattening us up," and Dad fixed the car. After spending four months in evangelism on the west coast and making appeals for our Kentucky missions work, we were ready to return to "our land."

On our trip back to Kentucky, we stopped to visit friends in Iowa. While we were there, I sensed a need to touch God as never before. The burden for souls was overwhelming. My vision had been growing beyond the mountains of Kentucky and was now reaching around the world. I wasn't sure what the Lord was trying to tell me, but I urgently needed to find a place to be alone with Him.

I looked across the street and noticed a vacant house. Suddenly, I knew what I had to do. I called Barbara into the room and gestured out the window. "Barbara, I'm going to that house across the street. I have to get alone with God and find His perfect will, and I'm going to pray and wait before God until I have an answer. Don't come and get me because I'm not going to leave until I hear from Him."

With determination, I walked across the street. I entered the front door and said aloud, "God, You're either going to have to answer me or they'll find a skeleton in this house." At that particular moment, knowing the will of God was more important to me than life itself.

During the next three days and nights, I sought God's will. I did not eat during that time. The hunger for God's perfect will was greater than my craving for food. My desire to do more for God was insatiable. I wanted to help more and more people.

After many hours of praying, meditating, and reading my Bible, I finally felt the assurance that my prayers had been heard. From that moment, a dramatic change occurred in my life.

The Lord said in Jeremiah 33:3, "Call unto me and I will answer thee, and shew thee great and mighty things, which thou knowest not." King David said, "Wait on the Lord: be of good courage" (Psalm 27:14). I guess I always felt He had heard my prayers, I just hated to wait.

Chapter Twelve

DOWN THE SAWDUST TRAIL

My old car looked like a porcupine with poles and long tent stakes sticking out the windows, tied on the sides, and protruding from the trunk. As I drove down Main Street with a huge mound of canvas bound on the roof, I must have provided a comical sight for the people of Hazard. They all stopped what they were doing and lined the streets to watch our arrival back home. Anything unusual provided entertainment, and I was a one-man parade.

Laughter filled the crowd, but I didn't mind. I planned to get a lot of people saved in that little twenty-by-forty-foot army hospital tent. It had been used to heal people physically before, and I figured it would provide a place for the Spirit of the Lord to operate on souls.

God had met me in that abandoned house in Iowa with a new vision and surge of power. Before we arrived back in Hazard, I had been conducting open air crusades with new vigor. The crowds had grown tremendously. When I heard about a tent for sale in South Carolina, I knew the time had come to put the first stage of my dream into reality.

I pitched that tent in remote areas throughout the mountains. Hundreds who had never been reached found the Lord. We filled local churches and helped establish new ones where there was no church for the new converts.

Contagious Faith

Down by the river, I found a heavily wooded place where I could commune with God. He was teaching me the importance of praying in His will, and I was learning to trust Him with complete confidence.

One morning while tramping along the wooded track from our trailer down to my prayer spot, I suddenly felt a sharp stabbing pain in my foot. A rusty nail had pierced my foot and was sticking out through the top of my shoe. I limped back home, bleeding freely from the wound. Trying to keep my mind off the pain, I decided to go over to the little church we still pastored to do some cleaning. While walking around outside, I stepped on another nail with the other foot.

I'm going to trust God, I thought. In spite of everything, it's going to be all right.

I crossed the open field beside the church to check the progress of the men who were setting up my tent for a crusade scheduled for that evening. As I walked past a pile of tent stakes, a copperhead snake bit my leg. The men putting up the tent heard my surprised yell.

"Brother Ken, you need to get that taken care of right away," they warned in unanimous agreement.

"No, I'll just trust the Lord!" I said.

"Man, you'll die!"

I heard them muttering in the background about all the things that had happened to me that day. Some felt that if I didn't die from snakebite, I would surely die from lockjaw.

"God, you healed others, and you can heal me," I prayed as I still sat on the ground. By now my leg was swelling, and the pain was mounting in intensity.

The men walked over to me and remarked, "Ain't no need to finish setting up this tent now. There won't be any service."

Since I refused to go to the hospital, they felt they could do nothing more, so they left. At that moment I was in too much pain to do any persuading.

"God," I said, "if You called me, then You'll heal me. Either faith works or it doesn't." (Unless God speaks directly to you, I advise getting medical help in similar emergencies.)

I got up and finished setting up the tent myself, and the swelling and pain left. By that evening, word about my healing had spread. Out of curiosity, people arrived at the meeting to see a man who had suffered several serious injuries with no ill effects.

After seeing the miracle and hearing the Word, many people responded to the altar call. A lady with a goiter the size of a large melon on the side of her neck came up for prayer. I reached out to touch her, and the effect was like sticking a pin in a balloon. The goiter shrank in front of our eyes. Shouts of "Praise the Lord" and "Hallelujah" filled the tent.

I was surprised to see the local deputy sheriff next in line.

"Preacher, I can't hear well out of one ear and can't hear at all in the other. I need my hearing. Seeing the miracles and how God healed you, I believe God will heal me, too, if you pray." He had great faith. When I touched him, God opened his ears.

The next night the sheriff was back in the healing line. "I thought you got healed last night," I said.

"Yeah, preacher. But I want you to pray for God to tone it down. I can hear so good I ain't got used to it yet. The noise bothered me so much I couldn't sleep last night."

I laughed along with the crowd. Not knowing any better, I laid my hands on his forehead and said, "God, make him a little deaf so it won't bother him, and he can still hear some."

The demands for our ministry increased. Churches in many cities and states extended invitations for us to come to their area. Soon the small tent with its seating capacity of only two hundred could no longer accomodate the crowds. Scores stood around the perimeter to hear the Word of God and witness the miracles He performed.

I was not a healer. But I followed the direction of God's Word, laid my hands on people, and prayed that God would touch them. God honored His Word, and many miracles took place.

Deuteronomy 11:26-28 says, "Behold, I set before you this day a blessing and a curse; A blessing, if ye obey the comandments of the Lord. . .and a curse, if ye will not obey."

I simply tried to obey the Lord and bless other people. The more I blessed them, the more God blessed me.

Chapter Thirteen

RAISE THE BRIDGE

Pulling the eight-by-thirty-foot house trailer behind us, Barbara, Nathan, and I left Hazard to expand our ministry. Our small tent had been sold, and we were filled with great expectations as we embarked on our newest evangelistic endeavors.

In July, 1958, I returned to Hazard auditorium to hold a revival. The crowds were tremendous, and hundreds were saved and healed. Although we had been traveling all over Kentucky, we planned to be back in Hazard when Barbara gave birth to our second child. Our son, Dan, was born on March 12, 1959.

After locating a larger tent for our crusades, we began to travel again. Our first out-of-state invitation came from Gallipolis, Ohio. People from the tri-state area of Ohio, West Virginia, and Kentucky filled our tent to overflowing. Many miracles took place and families were restored. One family brought their blind mother to the meeting, and she walked out seeing perfectly. A hemophiliac (bleeder) was healed. Cancers and diabetes disappeared.

After that crusade, we felt it was time to begin tent evangelism across the country. We scheduled our crusades so we could arrive in Washington with my parents when Barbara gave birth to our third child.

In Sedalia, Missouri, a crowd of over six hundred people filled the tent for our crusade. I grew excited; but I was also confused when only two people responded to the altar call. "God, you promised miracles and souls. You promised success."

On the second night of the crusade, a young mother brought her little two-year-old blind girl up to the platform for prayer. I wondered, Boy, God, you really wanted to give me a chance to test my faith, didn't you?

I laid my hands on her and commanded, "Blindness, in the name of Jesus, I cast you out."

The little girl began to cry and then turned to look at her mother for the first time in her young life. I don't think there was a dry eye in the tent. Seventy-five sinners found their way down the sawdust trail that night and wept their way through to a clean new life.

Several other outstanding miracles took place in that meeting. What a thrill we all had as a young boy began to walk for the first time in his life! He had been unable to stand erect since birth.

One woman was brought to the service from the hospital. Her abdomen had bloated to such proportions that she looked as if she would burst. Compassion overwhelmed me. When someone told me she was dying, I looked at her and said, "If I am God's servant, He is going to heal you."

I marveled at my boldness. "God, You'd better hear me!" I prayed silently.

In an instant the swelling disappeared, and the woman's belt and skirt dropped to the floor. She looked down with both embarrassment and elation. A murmur rose from the audience. Those in the rear stood on their seats to get a better view of the miracle. Thankfully, she did have a slip on. Sheepishly, I said, "See, what did I tell you?"

Although I had attended Bible school, I still had much to learn about proper pulpit etiquette. When I prayed in those days, I felt I had to pray long and hard. I would contort my face and scream loudly so that God would hear me and answer my prayers.

In one crusade a man came up to me and said, "Pray for me. I have *catarrh* (a nasal disorder)."

Thinking he said he had a guitar, I replied, "Well, bring it out and play it."

God was patient with me, however, and honored my sincerity and faith. He soon sent other workers to share our vision and help carry our burden for souls.

We began to publish *Faith In Action,* a bi-monthly magazine filled with testimonies, news, and our crusade schedule. Jim and Jane joined us to help with the magazine and act as crusade directors. We needed their help in many ways, for the problems that beset a crusade ministry are endless and exhausting.

Miracle Over The Ohio

During a terrible storm in Iowa, we lost our tent and organ—along with the offering—but managed to salvage the side curtains. We pieced them together with another tent that we bought, creating a sixty-by-one-hundred-twenty-foot tent. By purchasing a big furniture truck to haul the tent and equipment, we were able to use it for storage during the winter months when cold weather prevented outdoor meetings. We held church and auditorium services during those months. Most of the time either Jim or I drove the tent truck ahead of our other vehicles so we could set up before the others arrived.

When we left a meeting in West Virginia, a fellow minister accompanied me to our next crusade in Ohio. Trying to make time, I was driving the truck along at a pretty good clip when we began our descent down a long hill.

My friend had been fairly quiet for the last ten or fifteen minutes. As we neared the Ohio River, he startled me when he suddenly sat straight up. Looking at the road ahead, his terror-filled voice began shouting, "Stop! Stop! Stop!"

We were fast approaching a steel bridge that spanned the river. Unable to determine the reason for his excitement, I slammed on the brakes. But it was too late! With all the weight we were hauling, the mechanical brakes were inadequate to stop us in time. The momentum carried us through the yawning entrance of the bridge.

"Oh, no!" he sobbed as he slid down in the seat and nearly fainted.

The low girders overhead passed by in a blur. Finally, the truck rolled to a stop on the other side of the bridge. Still puzzled, I looked at the preacher and saw he was still shaking and could not speak; so I got out to see what caused his alarm.

I walked to the rear of the truck and looked up in amazement. *The truck was too tall for the bridge!* By this time the preacher had regained control and joined me. "Ken," he said, "you've got to see this!"

Following him across to the other side of the bridge,

he pointed at the sign that had caused his fear. The sign read, "Danger, low overhead, 10 feet, 6 inches."

"That's what I tried to tell you," he said.

The truck was 11 feet, 6 inches high and also had a little carrier mounted on top of the cab. To prove to ourselves beyond a doubt, I put the truck in reverse and tried to back under the bridge. The truck wouldn't go under.

"Ken," he said, "don't tell this story for awhile because people will surely think we're crazy!"

Then I remembered that the Bible is full of unusual, fantastic, hard-to-believe stories—water turned to wine, people raised from the dead, an ocean that parted down the middle, a man that walked on water, and, can you believe, a donkey that *talked.*

The Bible states in 2 Corinthians 5:7, "For we walk by faith, not by sight." Hebrews 11:6 says, "Without faith, it is impossible to please Him." So, I guess it's not too hard for God to raise a bridge or lower a truck.

Chapter Fourteen

RECKLESS FAITH

We were introduced as "America's Most Unique Gospel Team." Seven-year-old Nathan sang, preached, and played banjo and bass guitar. Dan, four, sang and played the drums. Becki, born two years before on September 23, 1960, captured everyone's heart as she sang and played a tambourine. Some nights Becki would lead the song service just like an adult. Barbara played the organ and accordion, and I played the guitar and trumpet and preached.

When we were on the road, Barbara was not only the mother but teacher as well. She taught the children their school subjects, music, and Bible. At four years of age, Nathan could quote over one hundred Bible verses *with references.*

Our crowds grew larger, and so did our crusade team. When Cecil joined us, he became my right-hand man. He had given up a career in the business world to be our temporary tent manager, organist, and business manager.

The addition of Bill in 1962 to our team was truly a blessing. A former Ringling Brother Circus roustabout and tent manager, he took over the job of managing the tent, which left Cecil free to concentrate on his music and the business aspect of our ministry.

We needed a professional like Bill to oversee the erection of our new ninety-by-one-hundred-ninety-foot tent. It seated three thousand people and took two days to set up.

A Fearful Descent

Transporting all our equipment was not without perils. The two tractor-trailers were often in need of repair, and mechanical failures occurred.

While driving through Idaho, we approached a long twelve-mile, downhill grade. Arnie, our public relations man and part-time musician was driving. This particular stretch of road was dangerous due to the hazardous curves. When I noticed our speed, I was concerned.

"Arnie, don't you think seventy is a little too fast to go down this hill?" I asked, watching the trees and shrubbery whizzing by in a blur. Looking at his face, I could see his tenseness and the nervous perspiration beading on his forehead.

"I know, Ken," he said, "but I've been trying to slow down. The brakes are gone. I'm trying, but I can't help it!"

"Well," I said, trying to remain calm as I watched the speedometer needle inch further toward the right, "gear the thing down!"

Slamming in the clutch, he strained at the gearshift. "It won't budge!" His efforts were in vain. "Ken, it won't move out of gear!"

I tried to help him, but it was impossible to disengage

the gears. He pulled the emergency brake, and I looked back to see smoke billowing from the dual wheels, which continued to roll without resistance.

"Ken, I'm afraid! I can't do anything with this thing. You'd better take over!" he pleaded.

I looked at the speedometer, which now registered eighty miles an hour, and yelled, "Let me over!"

I kept my eyes on the road and stuck my legs over the gearshift, grabbing the wheel. Arnie slid under me. We experienced a moment of panic when I couldn't get over and he couldn't get out from under me.

The needle climbed steadily. The truck weaved back and forth across the road while we changed places. Finally reaching the passenger's side, Arnie shrieked, "Ken, you can't stop this! I'm gonna jump out!"

"Don't do that! You'll be killed," I pleaded as I fought for control of the vehicle.

Knowing our lives could be over any moment, I thought, I should have written a book about all the crazy things that have happened to me. Now it's too late!

As we steadily built up speed, the trailer tried to jack-knife rounding the curves.

"What if we meet someone?" Arnie yelled.

"Why did you say that?" I said as I suddenly saw a Greyhound bus come into view up ahead. I only had a split second to decide which way to go. If I hit this bus, we'll die! If I pass it and meet someone else head on, we're gonna die. *We're gonna die either way!* I concluded.

"Maybe no one is coming," I said aloud and turned the steering wheel to pull around the bus at about ninety miles per hour. The people stared out the bus windows in astonishment. The big truck was vibrating so violently I felt we would soon shake apart. We could hear the high-pitched whining as all eighteen tires joined together in their eerie singing.

Finally, we reached the bottom and coasted to a stop. Quite shaken at the ordeal, Arnie and I cast relieved glances at one another. We jumped down from the cab onto unstable legs to examine the truck for any signs of damage. As the Greyhound bus roared past, the driver blew his big air horns and shook his head.

Once again, if God hadn't taken care of us with His protecting power, we would have been killed. He had overridden our mistake in not gearing the truck down at the top of the hill. We simply had to trust Him and ask Him to give us better sense the next time.

Serving A Big God

Someone once asked me, "Ken Gaub, with all those trucks, cars, trailers, tent equipment, radio broadcasts, magazines, and employees to pay, don't you get scared?"

Laughing, I replied, "As far in debt as I am, I can't afford to get scared. I'm serving a big God! I'm not letting up, stopping, or quitting. *He'll* take care of the people and equipment."

God has proved His protection time and time again. When we were holding a crusade in Sioux Falls, South Dakota, the radio news announced a tornado was coming through the area. Having lost one tent in a storm already, we were concerned. Bill told me, "Ken, I have an idea that might work."

"Let's try it. It's better than nothing!" I agreed.

Men from sponsoring churches pitched in and worked frantically to lash the huge tent to the two semis that we had manuevered into a "V" shape. Then we prayed for God's mighty protection as winds of seventy to ninety miles an hour whipped through the town.

The following day, a news crew from the local TV station came out to film the big top still standing amid the rubble of buildings that had collapsed all around it.

I even got in on the news unintentionally. Seeing the newsmen's car rolling downhill from its parking place, I gave chase. The cameramen were so busy they didn't notice it at first. As I leaned in through the window, half in and half out, and pulled the brake, they turned the cameras on me and recorded it for "posterity."

Besides protecting us from many disasters, God also continued to bless us in other ways. Taking a mental inventory of God's blessings one day, I recalled the time I told my mother, "One of these days I'll have a tent and help people just like Oral Roberts."

Inside our tent, we placed a wooden ramp in front of the platform so the sick could pass before me just as I had seen in Oral's crusade years before. During the service, Bill pushed a man in a wheelchair up the ramp and stepped back. But he failed to take the precaution of locking the brakes on the wheelchair, and it began to roll down the other side of the ramp. Before we could stop it, the chair hit the bottom and threw the man out. Seeing him lie there, I cried aloud, "God, you've either got to heal this man or he'll die." The man stood to his feet perfectly whole and walked back up the ramp where a red-faced evangelist and his assistant joined him in praising God.

In that same meeting, an eleven-year-old boy who had been unable to utter a sound since birth received healing and perfect speech.

With unwavering faith in the power of God, I often made seemingly brash statements. A small boy, wearing braces attached to special shoes, was helped to the platform by his parents. I could see the hope in their eyes. Motioning to the boy, I proclaimed to the audience, "If I'm God's servant, this boy will walk. If not, I'm a false prophet, and he will not walk."

I still have those braces hanging in my office to confirm that miracle.

Barb was sometimes reluctant to give full approval to my bold ventures. She would appeal to my sense of reason. "Ken, you're always quick to jump into something and then think about it a week later."

Often, when I would realize my mistake too late, she would say matter-of-factly, "Well, you've done it now. You'll just have to live with it!"

That usually made me feel uncomfortable. Yet, I knew she supported me, and I don't ever remember her interfering. She had confidence in my commitment to the work of the Lord. If I claimed anything from God, she believed I had faith enough to believe it would happen.

Newspaper articles often called me a flamboyant promoter. In our advertisements, we offered "One Way Ambulance Services." At one of our crusades, some members of a family got a court order to get their mother out of the hospital and bring her to the service. The family dispute had been reported to the press, and crowds showed up to see the outcome.

Stern-faced unbelievers sat there with a "Well, show

us!'' look on their faces. The situation was critical. Looking at the wrinkled, helpless little woman lying on the stretcher in front of me, I said within myself, God, either you heal this lady or *I might as well pack up and go home.*

Thankfully, God spared both of us. The woman rose from the stretcher completely healed.

What a thrill when Nathan came up to me after the service and said, "Dad, I get a good feeling on the inside when you pray for people that get healed like that lady on the cot."

The responsibility of praying for the sick was serious business, but often things happened that had a comical side to them. During one meeting, an elderly black lady came for prayer. A little, black net covering her stiffly sprayed hair was almost invisible. After praying for her, she walked away and a bald-headed man moved into place. As I laid my hand on his head, I didn't realize that the hair net had stuck to my hand. The ripple of laughter among the crowd made me look up and notice him walking away with the hair net clinging to his bald head.

Reaching Out

As the miracles continued, new opportunities to expand our ministry began to surface. Because I like to use the word "faith" in everything, we named our radio program, *The Active Faith Hour.* We broadcast fifteen weekly programs across eight states—including Alaska—and the Congo, Luxembourg, and Bangkok. Our *Faith In Action* magazine was sent throughout the United States and into forty-four foreign countries.

Our personal ministry had reached across thirty-nine states, but the flame of evangelism still burned in me for the "uttermost parts of the world." Some pastors in Ireland had become acquainted with me through the *Faith In Action* periodical, and when we received an invitation from them, Barbara and I wanted very much to go.

"How can we go?" we wondered. Someone suggested *S & H Green Stamps*. Churches and individual supporters began saving the stamps to finance our trip. In a matter of months, they had donated the necessary number of books filled with stamps. The trading stamps were exchanged for cash, and we bought tickets to the British Isles.

With a tearful goodbye, we left our children with my parents and boarded our first overseas jetliner, a Boeing 707 operated by British Overseas Airlines Company.

After nearly a month of ministry in a dozen countries, we arrived back in the United States exhilarated. The same kind of miracles we had witnessed in our homeland were performed by the power of God on foreign soil.

I think of the thousands of missionaries who have left family and friends for the sake of the gospel and sacrificed to preach God's Word on foreign soil. Romans 12:1-2 says we are to present our bodies as a "living sacrifice" that we may prove what is "that good, and acceptable, and perfect, will of God."

If you know it's God's will to take a short missionary trip—or a long overseas missions venture—God will bless and anoint you. Don't let fear hold you back. Take a step of faith, and let the Lord prove His love as He guides and protects you in response to your obedience.

Chapter Fifteen

NOT BARBARA, LORD

Near Mt. Zion in Jerusalem, Israel, is a spot sacred to Jews, Moslems, and Christians alike. It is Mt. Moriah, where the patriarch Abraham met his greatest test of faith when he offered his only son, Isaac, on an altar as a sacrifice to God.

In Mt. Zion, Illinois, I met the greatest test of faith in all my ministry. Barbara lay unconscious, dying of cancer in a four-bed ward of City Hospital.

Early in 1963, Barbara began to experience difficulty in her monthly menstrual cycle. Extreme hemorrhaging drained the strength from her body, leaving her tired and weak. She was not her usual outgoing, vibrant, positive self.

Barbara had never been one to complain, so she put on a bold front and acted as if nothing were wrong. She carried on her everyday duties as usual, tending to the demands of three young children, helping with the business of our crusades, and singing and playing her accordion every night in the services.

Although we prayed many times, her condition grew steadily worse until she finally consented to see a doctor. We were in a tent crusade in Rockford, Illinois, at the time.

No hint in the doctor's face or his tone of voice suggested to Barbara that she had anything to be seriously concerned about as he examined her.

"Well, Barbara," the doctor stated, "I believe that the examination has been satisfactory. You will be okay."

Immediately after Barbara left his office, however, the doctor telephoned me. "Mr. Gaub, I'm calling you about your wife's condition."

"Is something wrong, doctor?" I asked.

"Mr. Gaub, I'm afraid I have some bad news. Your wife has cancer," he replied.

"Is there anything you can do?" I was stunned.

"I'm terribly sorry, but the cancer has progressed to the final stages. It's inoperable."

I couldn't believe it. "How long does she have, doctor?"

"That's hard to say, but I'd guess about thirty days. I'm sorry, Mr. Gaub."

At first the words of the doctor were like a great weight dropping into my heart. My blood chilled in my veins as a great sigh of despair issued from deep within.

I managed a feeble, "Goodbye, doctor." My mind was in a frantic whirl of uncertain thoughts. God, this can't be! I pleaded in my spirit. I've preached faith. People are healed through my ministry. Why would you take my wife from me?

Then faith began to emerge from all the tangled confusion of human reasoning and emotions. God, I've said before that if you're not big enough to take care of me and my family, then there is no reason to preach the gospel. But, God, you have proven in the past that you can. Lord, I'll just have to trust you now.

When Barbara arrived back at the motel, I tried to act as natural as possible to keep her from knowing what the doctor had said.

The revival crusade continued in Rockford, with great miracles being performed by the power of God each night. Scores of men, women, boys, and girls surrendered their lives to Jesus Christ.

Miracle-working faith remained strong in every service we held, but Barbara grew steadily worse. She hemorrhaged heavier every day and spent most of her time resting. Although she was in such pain that she never felt comfortable, at each evening service she somehow summoned enough strength to minister to others.

When the Rockford crusade came to a close, we dismantled the huge tent cathedral and loaded it along with all our equipment into the big tractor-trailers. Cecil drove the bus from which we did our radio broadcasts. On Wednesday, Barbara, the three children, and I went on ahead in the car, pulling our office trailer to the next city, Zion, Illinois. We were scheduled to begin nightly tent crusade services the following Friday night.

The two-and-a-half-hour drive from Rockford to Zion took its toll on Barbara. By the time we arrived, she could hardly sit upright. She had barely spoken the entire trip, and the color in her face was gone. Three-and-a-half-year-old Becki didn't understand why her mommy couldn't hold her.

Immediately upon arrival in the city of Zion, I called the sponsoring pastor of the scheduled crusade, Rev. Gaye Brown, and told her of Barbara's condition. She sensed the concern in my voice.

"You'd better get her to a hospital right away," she

urged. "I'll call ahead to let them know you are coming."

Without taking time to unhook the trailer from the car, I drove straight to the emergency ward of the hospital. Having been advised of our imminent arrival by Pastor Brown, a staff of nurses and a resident doctor were on hand to give immediate attention to Barbara's critical needs. The highly skilled professional crew went into action.

An internist began to check her vital signs. In a half-conscious state, Barbara's breathing was labored and irregular. Her pulse rate was high as her heart beat desperately to pump the small amount of blood left in her body. The doctor described her blood pressure as "next to nothing."

Pastor Brown's personal physician arrived shortly thereafter. He was compassionate and concerned yet very professional. Allowing me to stay in the room as nurses drew a curtain around Barbara's bed, the middle-aged Jewish doctor prepared for further examination. As he poked and probed Barbara's abdominal area, she awoke to full consciousness because of the intense pain. I could tell from the look on the doctor's face that the situation was grave.

Beckoning to me, the doctor walked out of the room. I followed him into the wide hallway. "Mr. Gaub," the doctor said softly, "your wife is in extremely critical condition. I regret to inform you that most probably she will not last through the night."

Stunned by the thought of losing my wife, I returned to Barbara's bedside. She was under sedation but still suffering unbearable pain.

The Touch Of Faith

Sometime around nine o'clock that evening, Barbara lost total consciousness. For a time it seemed that life was nearly gone from her frail body. About half an hour had slowly passed when she surfaced to consciousness. Slowly, her eyelids opened, and she saw me standing over her.

"Ken, pray for me," she pleaded weakly.

I took her hands in mine and prayed a prayer of last minute desperation. I don't remember the exact words I said, but somewhere down deep inside faith began to rise. God placed a calm assurance in my heart, and I knew I had touched His heart. I *knew* that Barbara was going to be healed.

Barbara sensed an indisputable release of faith at the very same moment. Even though she was fully aware of the seriousness of her physical condition by now, she had never once doubted that healing would come. Following that short, simple prayer, Barbara experienced no unusual signs to confirm her healing— no cold chills, hot flashes, goose bumps, or physical sign of a tumor being passed. She just knew that God had answered prayer. *The pain was gone. She was healed!*

"My wife has been healed!" I exclaimed to the surprised attendant at the nurses' station. Soon I had the whole ward and wing of the hospital in a commotion.

The head nurse tried to calm me. She thought maybe I needed some kind of sedation myself.

"But I *know* she's healed," I said. *"She's hungry!* She wants something to eat! Get her something!"

"I'm sorry," the nurse responded, "but I can't give

her any food unless the doctor authorizes it. Besides, the kitchen closed three hours ago."

"Get me the doctor then," I demanded.

At first the head nurse was reluctant to call the doctor back to the hospital; but, after my persistence, she finally consented.

The kindly Jewish doctor had just arrived at his home when the nurse summoned him back. Feeling that *I* needed him more than Barbara, he returned without delay. Barbara was sitting up in bed when the doctor walked into the ward. To satisfy me, he went through the motions of a partial examination, checking Barbara's pulse, blood pressure, and respiration.

He again motioned for me to follow him into the hallway.

"Mr. Gaub," he spoke matter-of-factly, "upon occasion a patient in your wife's condition will experience a remission of the symptoms of terminal cancer. But this is only temporary. We members of the medical profession don't have all the answers as to why this does happen."

"I know why!" I retorted. "*She's healed.* God healed her, and now she's hungry. I want you to see that she has some food."

The doctor agreeably asked the nurses to take food to Barbara. At that hour of the evening, however, the only food available was toast and hot tea. Barbara consumed them eagerly.

Before leaving the hospital again, the doctor reassured me, "If your wife really is healed as you believe, we will know in the morning. You'd better try to get some rest yourself," he further admonished.

Half-sitting and half-reclining in a chair by Barb's bed,

I extended my feet onto a small footstool. I rested well that night, enveloped by a peaceful assurance that the Great Physician had miraculously touched my wife and made her completely well.

The morning dawned, bringing with it even more evidence that what we believed had really happened. Barbara cleaned up every scrap of food on her breakfast tray and was still hungry.

The balding Jewish physician came through Barbara's ward while making his morning rounds. An extensive examination yielded no evidence of any cancer that only the night before had threatened to take my wife's life.

The doctor reluctantly admitted that everything seemed to be back to normal. But he felt that Barbara should remain in the hospital for further observation and tests.

The following day, Friday, Barbara wanted to be released from the hospital. The doctor insisted that she stay just to make sure everything was all right, even though all reports from the previous days' testing had returned negative.

"Who's paying the hospital bill?" I asked the doctor.

"You are," he replied bluntly.

"If I'm paying the bill, then I want her to be released *immediately!*"

The doctor complied with my wishes, and soon Barbara and I were walking joyfully arm-in-arm out of the hospital.

That very evening in the Zion crusade service, Barbara sang, played her accordion, and testified to the miraculous healing power of God. Her faith inspired the believers, and great signs, wonders, and miracles were performed in the name of Jesus Christ.

While relating this story and other miraculous experiences in our ministry to Dr. C.M. Ward, *Revival Time* radio preacher, he nicknamed me "Mr. Faith." I must admit, however, that much of the success of our ministry is due to the unfaltering faith of my wife, Barbara. If I deserve the title of "Mr. Faith," then surely she is "Mrs. Faith."

Isaiah 53:5 says, "With his stripes we are healed." Today, more than twenty years later, Barbara is still a beautiful picture of health. She has had no recurrence of symptoms and no problems at all of this nature. Hallelujah!

Chapter Sixteen

AROUND THE WORLD IN 101 DAYS

"What is your reason for going overseas?"

"Aren't there enough people in America who need the gospel?"

"Does God expect parents to leave their children behind?"

"Who is going to pay for it?"

"Is it really worth it?"

These and other questions were asked as we told about our planned trip around the world. The first overseas tour in December, 1963, only whetted my appetite for world evangelism. A compelling sense of urgency gripped me as I realized that millions of people around the world were dying every year without hearing the message of salvation. The words of Jesus Christ to "go into all the world and preach the gospel" seemed as mandatory to me as it did to the early apostles. (See Mark 16:15.)

Following our trip to Europe, we made every effort to acquaint others with the tremendous need to reach the lost with the Word of God. In our crusades and through our *Faith In Action* magazine, believers were urged to get involved in spreading the gospel. We devoted much space in our magazine to articles by overseas missionaries and appeals for their support. But the time came when I had to do more than promote missionaries—I had to become one.

Invitations to preach were received in our *Faith In Action* mailbox from many of the forty-four countries our magazine reached. The appeals of native pastors and missionaries exacted a response from me. God had opened the door to bring our ministry to their people, and it was up to me to go through it.

Those "faraway places with strange-sounding names" were calling me: Karachi, Djarkarta, Bangkok, Calcutta—names of places I had learned about in geography class took on new meaning. They were not just cities of bricks, mortar, steel, and glass but people with eternal souls who were dying without any hope of salvation.

With pencil, paper, world atlas, and globe, Barbara and I sat down to plan our around-the-world itinerary. "This will probably be the only time we will go around the world," I told Barbara. "But we will go once and try to bless as many people as we can."

Arnie, our public relations manager, was elated when I asked him and Mary, his wife, to join us as part of our team on our Round-the-World Missionary Tour. Arnie, a former U.S. Coast Guard chaplain turned school teacher, had been a close friend of mine since college days.

After carefully plotting our globe-circling route and confirming overseas meeting schedules, we contacted a travel agency. "These are the places we will be holding our gospel meetings and the dates we need to be there," I informed the lady travel agent.

Overwhelmed by our tight itinerary, she said, "It will take a miracle to schedule an airline flight each day you want one. On certain days, some of these countries don't even have flights."

"That's all right," I assured her. "We believe in miracles, so go ahead and book them."

Leaving our schedule with the travel agent, we trusted God to work everything according to His will. After several days, the agent called me on the telephone. "Mr. Gaub, I have your itinerary completed. Everything is as you wished."

"That's great!" I responded.

"You realize, of course, that this trip is going to cost a lot of money," she warned. "For all the airline flights, hotels, food, visas, taxes, and other expenses, it will cost you about ten thousand dollars."

"Fine," I said, "money is no problem."

Money was no problem—*I didn't have any.* But I knew we were obeying the will of God, and I was just as sure that He would provide the finances.

As we continued to minister across the country, we designated one service in each of our crusades and revivals as "Missions Night" and received an offering toward the expenses of the trip. In addition, an appeal went out through our magazine for financial support.

The travel agent began calling me about eight months before our departure date. As the day drew nearer, I sensed growing concern in her voice.

"Mr. Gaub, you know you're scheduled to begin your trip very soon, don't you?" she asked.

"I know," I replied. "I'm so excited, I can hardly wait!"

"I must ask you about the money for the trip," she

stated.

"Oh, don't worry about the money. It's coming," I assured her. "It's coming."

"Where is it coming from?" she asked.

"I don't know, I'm not God," I kidded. "I'll just pray. Maybe someone will give me $10,000. Maybe ten people will give me $1,000. Maybe forty thousand people will give me a quarter. Who knows? It will all work out."

Three days before the deadline, the funds still had not arrived. I tried unsuccessfully to borrow the money from the bank, but we kept believing God for a financial miracle.

About twenty-four hours before our scheduled flight, the telephone rang. "Mr. Gaub," the banker on the other end asked, "are you still planning to leave on the trip?"

"I certainly am!"

"Did you get the money yet?"

"No, but it has to get here soon. I'm leaving in one day."

"Well, I've decided I'm going to loan you the money. I have arranged to delay your first payment until after your return."

The trip itself was a fantastic success. God blessed us to minister and preach to thousands of foreign nationals and to lift and encourage missionaries all over the world. Miracles of healing took place, and many people found the Lord. We were certainly glad we took the step of faith.

When we returned home, God laid our debt on the hearts of certain people, and soon the loan was paid off. David said, "The Lord is my shepherd, I shall not want'' (Psalm 23:1) and ''They that seek the Lord shall not want any good thing'' (Psalm 34:10). God is true to His Word.

Chapter Seventeen

FAITH TRIED AND ALMOST DIED

Many people believed that the tent meeting was a part of vanishing Americana, along with county fairs and three-ring circuses. But God continued to bless and show us favor.

"We just keep getting bigger tents," I answered skeptics. In fact, the ninety-by-three-hundred foot tent I had at that time was only a year old and still in excellent condition.

In Mason City, Iowa, where I had worked in a grocery store as a youth, we held a meeting. Excited to be the hometown boy returning after all these years, I had great expectations for a sensational meeting. But I felt disappointed when the crusade ended. After all my bragging about God supplying our needs, I owed over $1,000, mostly to local businesses. The bills were due immediately, and we had no money to pay them.

Maybe I've missed God, I thought as I watched the tent being dismantled. Maybe I should give up evangelistic work and pastor some small country church.

Bowing my head, I prayed, "God help me." Once again I felt that familiar presence I had trusted so often.

Then my favorite Scripture verse came into my mind. Matthew 6:33 had been and continued to be the key to my entire life: *"Seek ye first the kingdom of God, and his righteousness; and all these things shall be added unto you."* I had been seeking Him and doing His will. He would add whatever we needed.

We had finished loading the equipment when a man who had attended our crusade walked up to me and handed me an envelope. He said, "God has told me to help you." The envelope contained the amount needed to pay the crusade costs. Tears of joy and gratitude flowed down my face.

Thank You, Lord, for adding these things unto us, I prayed inwardly as renewed determination stirred in my soul. God had confirmed He still wanted me out on the front lines of this great spiritual warfare. His love and concern for me would soon be shown in another way, too.

Grounded By God

Our next crusade was scheduled for Des Moines, Iowa. I had other business there and wanted to fly in ahead of the team. My friend, Don, who was working with us, had a pilot's license and offered to take me if I would rent the plane.

I paid the reasonable $12 rental fee, and we took the plane up for a test flight. Everything checked out, so we decided to take off the next morning.

As we headed for the airport the next day, I began experiencing some nausea. I told Don, "I don't think we can go this morning." So we turned around and began driving to Mason City. I felt fine, so we turned again to go back toward the hangar. I felt sick again, so this time we decided to drive. I began feeling better so I said, "Let's try it one more time."

We started back toward the airport, but this time Don got sick. I said, "I surely don't want a sick pilot. Don, maybe God doesn't want us to fly. We'll just drive to Des Moines."

Following the first evening service in Des Moines, I turned on the late news. "Don, come here," I called. "Listen to this! You've *got* to hear this!"

The news commentator reported, "The little Cessna 150, hired out of the Mason City hangar, crashed today just fifteen minutes out of the airport. The pilot and both passengers were killed instantly."

Don and I sat in stunned silence realizing that we had been miraculously spared from their fate.

David said in Psalm 91:1-2, "He that dwelleth in the secret place of the most High shall abide under the shadow of the Almighty. I will say of the Lord, He is my refuge and my fortress: my God; in him will I trust." To that I say, "*Amen*."

Once again God had protected me with His power. Otherwise, my friend and I may have been killed in that small plane. I believe that many times in our lives God protects us, and we don't even know it. Other times we do know. But we should always be thankful for God's protecting power. It pays to live for God.

Chapter Eighteen

WOUNDED IN ACTION

Bien Hra, Can Tho, Quang Ngai, Da Nang—names of Vietnam military bases I couldn't even pronounce were to become very important to me. The name of Da Nang stands out particularly in my mind. The warfare I encountered there was not spiritual—the bullets were real.

"Operation Vietnam" had been a burden upon my heart since visiting the U.S. servicemen and women on our first round-the-world missionary trip.

Thousands of New Testaments had been sent by our ministry to military personnel around the world. Their names were given to us by moms, dads, wives, and sweethearts we had met on our crusades and through our magazine. We enclosed a personal letter of encouragement with each New Testament, marking Scripture portions we felt would minister to individual needs.

Many heart-rending letters were received in our offices in Yakima, Washington. Here is an excerpt from one such letter that illustrates the importance of this particular ministry.

"Dear Ken Gaub:

You sent a New Testament to Charles Brewer from Oregon. Five minutes before he went to meet God, he prayed for me, and I, too, found God. I am keeping Charlie's New Testament. Thank you for thinking of us in Vietnam.

J.B. Andrews"

One of the "Operation Vietnam" New Testaments fell into the hands of the troupe that accompanied Bob Hope on his annual Christmas tour. We always enclosed our mailing address in each New Testament. My office was contacted in the fall of 1968, and I received an invitation to participate in the program when Mr. Hope visited our U.S. bases overseas.

Mixed emotions wrestled in my spirit. I was excited at the thought of having a part in the Bob Hope show, and I considered the opportunity to minister to our men and women in uniform both a sacred privilege and a patriotic duty. But the thought of leaving Barbara and the children behind and the uncertainty of personal safety in a war zone left me uneasy. I knew, however, that it was God's will for me to go, and He had promised in His Word to protect His own. Besides, I felt certain that civilians like myself would be kept out of battle areas.

We arrived in Saigon, capital of the Republic of South Vietnam, the week of Christmas, 1968. My schedule called for me to appear on the Bob Hope program in the evenings. I would sing, play the guitar, and give a short, spiritual message to the military personnel at each of the five bases we visited.

During the daytime I visited with chaplains at nearby military outposts in the vicinity of the bases where we were to perform. These dedicated men of God were serving both their Lord and their country in some unthinkable conditions.

Under Enemy Fire

One particular day will remain permanently emblazoned in my memory. I had concluded a visit with an army chaplain near the border of communist-controlled North Vietnam and was preparing to return to Da Nang for the evening Bob Hope show. The nerve-shattering explosions of bombs and shells erupted all around us. We boarded a military helicopter to make what was supposedly a short hop back to Saigon. I was the only civilian on board.

The whirring blades of the helicopter had barely lifted us twenty feet into the air when we came under enemy fire. A Viet Cong mortar round struck the revolving blades, throwing the helicopter out of control. A piece of shrapnel pierced the fuselage and grazed my chin, and the chopper plummeted to the ground as enemy machine-gun fire ripped through the cockpit. We were in an open rice paddy and very vulnerable to the deadly fire of our attackers. I scrambled for the safety of an open drainage ditch about two hundred yards away. Crouching low, I ran as fast as possible through the muddy field.

The unrelenting staccato of bullets from hidden machine guns sprayed the rice paddy. A bullet ripped through my right forearm and shattered the bone. Bleeding and clutching my arm, I managed to reach the safety of an irrigation ditch. My heart pounded heavily as I lay there. The soldiers who were on board the helicopter with me returned the fire. It seemed like a nightmarish eternity until reinforcements finally reached us and silenced the enemy guns.

Another helicopter arrived to carry the wounded to a nearby military hospital. After four or five hours, I was finally released in time for the evening show.

When it came time for me to appear on stage, I walked out with a bandage on my chin and my arm in a cast resting in a sling.

"I was planning to sing and play my guitar for you this evening," I said, "but I changed my mind."

The service men and women laughed and cheered. Bob Hope stood slightly offstage and scolded teasingly, "You just stick to the preaching! I'll tell the jokes around here."

The audience laughed enthusiastically again. But my humorous remarks were few that evening as I addressed the hundreds of G.I.'s sitting before me.

The realization that many of these men would never live to see their homeland again sobered me. Just that day I had seen many of their buddies lying face down in the cold, soggy rice paddies, while their blood mingled with standing puddles of water.

A sense of urgency gripped my heart as I realized that, for some of those in my audience, this was the first and last time they would hear the gospel. Many acknowledged their need of salvation, and I pressed them to commit their lives to Jesus Christ. A feeling of inadequacy welled up within me as I realized that many who did not repent that day would die on some remote battlefield and be lost for eternity.

Christmas week ended, and the Bob Hope entourage returned to the United States. Barbara greeted me at the Los Angeles airport, and I hugged her with my good arm. The plaster cast encasing my arm still hung in a sling about my neck.

News of my brush with death in Vietnam had already made the papers. My introduction at the service that evening at the Alhambra Assembly of God received a standing ovation.

The pastor stated in his introduction, "Ken Gaub, our speaker this evening, has just returned from Vietnam. He volunteered to go even though he didn't have to. You may have heard that he had a little mishap over there."

Embarrassed, I stood on the platform acknowledging the applause. We had a great meeting that evening, and the faith of the believers was not at all hindered by the sight of the cast on my arm.

The pastor stated, "Here is a guy who will go anywhere to preach the gospel if he has the opportunity."

Jesus said in Mark 16, "Go ye into all the world, and preach the gospel." This was given as a command, not a request that you can decide whether or not you want to obey. God will honor you as you obey Him.

Maybe your "world" is not overseas. Maybe it's right in your hometown—your next-door neighbor, the person you work with, or your own family. But God will honor you as you witness for Him. Think about it.

Chapter Nineteen

CHANGING WITH THE TIMES

I have always enjoyed listening to other preachers and observing their methods. Billy Graham's ministry of emphasizing salvation to lost souls had a great influence on me. Oral Roberts influenced me by his emphasis of praying for the sick and ministering to the physical needs of believers. The positive preaching principles as proposed by Robert Schuller also became a part of my presentations. I urged people to have big faith in a big God.

To promote my crusades, I often used catchy titles for my messages to arouse curiosity and stir interest. Some of my favorites were, "Hair Cut in the Devil's Barber Shop" (the story of Samson and Delilah), "Seven Ducks in a Muddy River" (the healing of Naaman), and "Who is the Anti-Christ?" (I didn't know either).

I liked to preach on hell to attract college-age kids and teens. Knowing they like to make extra money, I would get their attention by offering a $1000 cash reward to anybody who could prove me wrong in a message titled, "Where Hell Is Located!" After a salvation appeal, I would give the answer, "Hell is located at the end of an ungodly life."

Once in a great crusade in Mansfield, Ohio, I invited Rex Humbard to join me. When we pitched the big top there in an area-wide crusade, I wanted this highly respected man of God on my platform more than anyone else.

Rex preached the opening night, and the Cathedral Quartet sang. I could not have been more honored.

While we were in Mansfield, a storm extensively damaged our big tent. God was still doing mighty miracles in our tent crusades, but the continued cost of operating our vehicles and equipment grew more prohibitive. We found ourselves called to auditorium meetings more and more, and the effectiveness of tent ministry began to decline. We had to change with the times.

We needed a less cumbersome means of carrying on our ministry. After selling our old Cadillac and trailer home, we moved into a used bookmobile. Cecil and I spent many hours adapting it to our needs. It had passenger seats up front, bunks in the middle, and an office area in the rear. We applied several coats of paint to cover the pink flowers that had decorated the walls. There wasn't room to put a bath in the bookmobile. I never got used to shaving with Ajax from the soap dispensers at gas stations or taking sponge baths in service station sinks when we couldn't afford motels or didn't have another place to stay.

Our ministry took yet another unexpected turn when we met Kash, a tour promoter and preacher from South Lebanon, Ohio. He invited us to become associate tour hosts on his Holy Land Tours. A love for Israel had taken root in our hearts. To walk in that holy and historic land meant much to me, and I felt it would be spiritually enriching to believers accompanying us. We could also offer trips to visit other nations for those who wanted to be part of our crusade team.

When an opportunity was presented for an open-air meeting in Barbados, a West Indies island in the Caribbean, we scheduled the first gospel meeting ever held on the north end of the island. Some people said, "We don't think this is a good place. It won't work. You won't get results here."

But people came by the thousands for two weeks, proving that God is a miracle-working God. As the evening shadows fell, men, women, boys, and girls from all walks of life made their way to the big soccer field where we held our crusade. They came by donkey cart, bicycles, trucks, buses, and a few cars. Many used the most common mode of transportation on the island—they walked. The city of Bridgetown cooperated by extending its bus service for the crusade.

The president of Barbados sent two men from the government to officially open our service. Later, we met the president himself at the radio station where we did our crusade broadcast.

Meeting with such success placed a deep burden in our hearts and compelled us to return. We planned more extensive campaigns in other cities and islands like Caracas, Trinidad, Barbados, Martinique, Guadalupe, and Curacao.

A heavy downpour in Trinidad on the opening night of the crusade caused no small concern to the sponsoring pastors. As we approached the crusade site, we saw thousands of people had already arrived from all over the islands. Their hearts were hungry to hear the gospel and to see the power of God demonstrated.

Because of the heavy rainfall, the first service seemed doomed to an early dismissal.

"Ken, what will we do? The rains have begun. Should we send the people home?"

With an inspired boldness, I walked up to the microphone and bowed my head. "Let's pray. God, if I'm Your servant, let it quit raining in one minute. Another thing, Lord, it may rain a lot here, but it won't rain after twelve o'clock noon for the next ten days until this crusade is over."

The drizzle slowed and then stopped. The clouds overhead dissipated. All that could be heard was rejoicing and praise as the people lifted up their hands toward the heavens and worshipped God.

God had brought our team to this nation at a very opportune time. Just days before, violence had left its mark on buildings downtown. Protest demonstrations, molotov cocktails, and riots were common. Political unrest had also dampened the air, and racial strife threatened the unsettled island. The country remained under a state of emergency.

But night after night the Word of God, mixed with music and song, blessed thousands of souls in Trinidad. Scores of people accepted Jesus for the first time. Bodies were healed, and families were reunited. The whole nation felt the impact of God's presence.

We visited hospitals, held meetings in schools and on college campuses, and spoke on the radio. Hundreds of youth came to God. Religious barriers broke as Moslems and Hindus surrendered to the Lord. An excerpt from a letter we received shows the impact:

"I was a Hindu, but the first night of

the Crusade, when you prayed and the rain stopped, made me realize your God is real. I gave my life to Him, and now I have joy and happiness, too. I love you all and want you to pray for me."

T.R.

After the crusade was over, one of the pastors escorted me to the airport. As I stepped out of the car to go into the airport, drops of rain splattered on the sidewalk.

The pastor smiled, "Ken, it's a good thing you didn't have one more night."

"I would have asked God to extend the time," I replied.

Crusades around the world brought us into contact with various missionaries who were giving their lives on foreign soil for Christ. Challenging people to help support them became a cause for us. We needed more men with unselfish devotion. Our hearts were touched with the work being done in India, and support of a children's home in Korea and missionaries in Africa and the Philippines became our own personal projects. We found delight in helping young preachers get a start. As we learned to give more and help other ministries, God gave more and more to us.

Within a year we realized our growing children and growing ministry had outgrown the old bookmobile. We bought a used 1950 Greyhound that was thirteen feet longer than the old bus. After selling all but two of the passenger seats, Cecil and I once again tackled the job of making a bus livable. The Greyhound had the added luxury of air conditioning, two-way radio, a telephone, and, best of all, a bathroom.

When you buy used equipment, you're never sure how long it will hold up. One day we were on our way through Grant's Pass, Oregon, when the bus engine blew. After getting towed to a service station, we rented a motor home in order to meet our schedule.

Between meetings, Cecil and I pulled the engine out, borrowed a pickup truck, and hauled the engine to Los Angeles for the necessary repairs. But on our way to the repair shop, something unexpected happened. I glanced to my left and saw a Volkswagen run a red light at an intersection.

I realized we were going to collide, so I accelerated to get out of the way. But when the pickup lunged forward, the engine fell off the bed and landed in the path of the oncoming Volkswagen. Needless to say, the Volkswagen hit the bus engine.

To make matters worse, a railroad track ran through the intersection. After getting the Volkswagen and driver clear, we heard the whistle of a train. Before we could get the bus engine out of the way, the train roared through the intersection, leaving mangled metal where the bus engine had been.

The only thing left to do was purchase a new engine with a price tag of several thousand dollars. But once again, God sent a financial miracle to put us back in our bus and on the road.

Deuteronomy 28:2 says, "All these blessings shall come on thee, and overtake thee, if thou shalt hearken unto the voice of the Lord thy God." When that train overtook my engine, I thought it was a disaster, but it ended up a blessing. God usually supplies something much better than what Satan has destroyed.

Matthew 6:33 says, "Seek ye first the kingdom of god, and his righteousness, and all these things shall be added unto you." One of my favorite promises is in Philippians 4:19: "My God shall supply all your need according to his riches in glory by Christ Jesus." God will turn negatives into positives, if your faith is in Him.

Chapter Twenty

HEAVEN

Traveling with a family, eating in restaurants, and teaching the kids their schooling on the road year after year was not easy. Yet we enjoyed it because we knew God had called us to this way of life. Our difficulty now was that the bus had become too small for our family. We had already lengthened the boys' bunk beds several times because they had grown so tall, and Becki could hardly squeeze into hers.

We needed a larger bus for leg room, eating room, and, certainly, a shower room. The greater demands for crusades also created a need for better transportation. I had my heart set on a particular make of bus that I had seen for sale. A majestic eagle with its wings full spread and head turned to the side graced the front of the bus. I knew we would have a smoother ride with a Silver Eagle because of its unique suspension system utilizing giant air-filled shocks. How I longed for a bus like that!

"God," I prayed, "You know we need the best equipment You can provide. We have millions of souls to reach."

Many of our friends dug deep into their pockets in

Christian love to help bring the miracle to pass. While we were in a crusade in Muskogee, Oklahoma, our big forty-foot Silver Eagle Trailways bus was delivered to us. Not only did we have better beds but a snack bar and a microwave oven. Barb even had room for her sewing machine.

When I opened up the luggage compartment doors beneath the bus, I found a wealth of storage space. We had never had so much room.

Destination: Glory

We wanted the bus to be a testimony during our travels, so we came up with a unique idea. To indicate our destination on the top front of the bus, we put the word "HEAVEN." It proved a bit startling to passersby.

Once when we were traveling through Mississippi, we saw a station wagon transporting a singing group of Nazarene college students blow a tire, flip over, and skid into our lane on its roof. We stopped to help and saw the boys climbing out the windows. One of them looked up and saw "HEAVEN" on our bus and nearly went into shock. In the excitement, he thought St. Peter had sent a bus to pick them up. One of the young men commented, "Man, this really makes you think seriously about eternity."

Truck drivers were especially fun to listen to. One of them said over the CB, "Man, I need a drink. I just saw a bus headed for *heaven*. Wonder who's driving that thing."

Unable to resist having fun, I picked up my CB and, using my "handle," said, "This is Saint Peter."

"Wow!" he said, "my wife won't believe this! Wait

until I tell her I saw a bus going to heaven and I talked to Saint Peter! You know, she's been praying for me."

Sometimes when we had extra time on our schedule, we picked up hitchhikers. One day with a big whoosh of the air brakes, I slowed the bus down, thrust open the door, and said, "Want a ride, buddy?"

The young man looked up at the sign that said "HEAVEN" and shook his head. "I don't have any money."

"I'm not asking you for money. Come on, get in," I said and motioned to him. He climbed in the bus and looked around, quickly taking everything in.

Curiosity got the best of him, and he asked, "What's with this 'heaven' sign?"

I replied, "That's where we are going!"

With all seriousness, he replied, "You're not going there today, are you?"

Witnessing to him was exciting, and I tried to explain what we were doing. He interrupted with, "Hey, who do you work for?"

I replied, "I work for God."

"Really? Well, how does He get a check to you?"

I laughed, and he continued, "Aren't you afraid when you pick up hitchhikers that they'll hold you up?"

"Naw!" I told him. "They don't hold *us* up—*we* hold up hitchhikers." That shook him until I explained, "I hold them in the bus until I tell them Jesus loves them."

We picked up another young man while traveling through North Dakota. He looked exhausted and was glad for a ride because he hadn't eaten anything for three days except a bag of Planter's Peanuts. At first, he felt reluctant to get on the bus.

Pulling into a truck stop, I said, "I'm going to buy you a meal."

He said, "No, I can't let you do that."

"Man, I can see that you're hungry."

On the brink of tears, he said, "But I can't do anything for you, and I don't have any money."

I finally persuaded him to go with me by telling him I needed something to eat, too. The waitress came over, pad in hand, and asked, "Well, what will it be?"

Seeing his hesitation, I said, "Order anything you want. If you want a milkshake, order it. If you want a hamburger, order it. If you want a T-Bone steak, order it." He ordered a milkshake, a hamburger, *and* a T-Bone steak!

He ate all the bread in the little basket on the table, drank several glasses of milk, and finally sat back feeling content. I realized he had really been starved.

Going back to the bus, I paused before getting on. "Now, remember, you don't have to do anything for me. You can go on your way now. If you want to keep riding with me, you have a ride."

He took one look at my smile and jumped back into the bus. A few minutes down the road, I led him to Jesus Christ. He couldn't believe how he felt. "Man, I've been on drugs and everything, but I've never been this high. Do you stay up here, or what happens when you come down?"

I instructed him further about his Christian walk, and he kept saying, "Wow!"

I began singing, "Thank you Lord, for saving my soul." He liked it and soon joined in with me.

"Did you know God is interested in every phase of your life?" I asked.

Shaking his head in amazement, he said, "I can't believe it. Just think, I stood out there for hours today, and nobody would give me a ride. I always get rides, but I didn't today until you came along."

I laughed and said, "God wanted me to pick you up, and you were out there so early that you had to wait for me."

"Wow, I can't get over it!" He shook his head in amazement.

"Well, God wanted me to meet you so I could lead you to Christ."

Continuing our conversation, we looked ahead and noticed another young man hitchhiking up ahead. I slowed down the bus and pulled alongside of him. My fellow passenger looked at me. "Are we going to do it to him, too?"

"Why not?" I grinned.

With a little encouragement from my first passenger, the boy got on. As I began chatting with the new one, the first one interrupted. He couldn't wait. "Man, has this guy got some things to tell you!"

But he didn't give me much of a chance and spilled out his new-found theology and experience. We soon led our new passenger to Christ also.

Gospel Gypsies

Hitchhikers weren't all we picked up—some things were more permanent. As we acquired more and more musical instruments and sound equipment, we found ourselves overcrowded again. But we trusted God to meet our needs, and two large donations were made toward the purchase of a Dodge Maxi-Van to transport our musical equipment.

By 1975, we had been on the road for twenty years. On that anniversary I realized, "Here I am a man without a home and a preacher without a church—a Gospel gypsy."

I knew that a lot of people thought we lived a life of glamour when they saw our bus and watched us perform on stage. Sure it was fun! But it was also work. We enjoyed it because God had called us to this way of life.

Traveling the highways and backroads of America has a way of wearing out buses. Soon our first brand new Silver Eagle replaced our old "Eagle." It was a thrill to be able to personalize our new bus the way we wanted it. Celebrity Coach in Nashville did the interior according to our precise instructions. We innovated a new idea—sinking the shower down into the body of the bus—that gave us an eight foot shower stall. Those tall boys of ours certainly needed that. The new bus was forty feet long with seven rooms, including four bedrooms, a kitchen, and an office. Of course, we continued to use "HEAVEN" on our destinator.

A little boy came up to me at one of our crusades. "You live in that bus?" he asked, eyes big with curiosity.

I said, "Yes."

Throwing his arms up with an exclamation, he yelled, "Wow! You live in a parking zone!"

I guess we have always lived like nomads, somewhat like a shepherd raising sheep out in the hills. We lead people to Christ, and they become His sheep. We help guide them into the fold, and then a local church helps them to grow in the ways of the Lord—while we continue traveling the globe finding more sheep.

Chapter Twenty-One

PLANE RIDES

"I'll ride in an airplane as long as I can keep just one foot on the ground," a prospective traveler once told me.

He was expressing a common fear in people who believe that flying is dangerous. But I have found it to be, by far, the safest mode of transportation and extremely convenient at times to meet the demands of my tight schedule.

A few times, though, I have been spared only through divine intervention.

During a flight from Seattle to Miami, my plane made a stop in Denver. For reasons unknown to me, the flight got rerouted back to Portland, Oregon. A mix-up in flight plans there kept me from making connections with a Miami flight.

Boarding another plane later in Portland, I leaned back, contented at finally being on my way. It seemed that I had to fly across the country twice to get to Florida. But when I closed my eyes in silent meditation and tryed to relax, the Lord said to me, *"Get off the plane!"*

I tried to get up without unfastening my seat belt.

"Excuse me," I said as I loosened the restraint and stepped into the aisle. Pushing past the passengers still in the process of finding their seats, I made my way to the exit. The stewardess looked startled as I ran back down the boarding ramp. I turned, smiled, and waved to her. The experience in Mason City, Iowa, had taught me something about planes—sometimes God doesn't want you on them.

I paused inside the terminal, watched the jet taxi down the runway, and then returned to the empty waiting room. I tried to sit down and collect my thoughts; but, after a few minutes, I got up and walked over to the airlines counter. The unsmiling clerk looked up.

"Excuse me," I said, "I missed my plane."

The counter attendant was unsympathetic and said sarcastically, "Why did you miss your plane?"

I shrugged and replied, "I wasn't on it."

"Why?"

"I can't tell you."

"Sir, why did you miss your plane?"

"Well," I smiled, "I was sitting in that chair over there."

Reaching for my ticket, he examined it. "Let me see. Well, Mr. Gaub, you can't go to Miami from here now. You'll have to go through San Francisco."

I felt as though I would have to fly all my life to get to Miami.

"Also," he continued, "there are no flights out tonight. Since you'll have to wait until tomorrow, you'd better try and find a motel room."

I gathered my luggage, left for the airport motel, and prayed silently as I walked. Well, Lord, here I am. I don't know why this is happening, but You do.

Soon I was sitting in a motel room, and I turned on the T.V. set. The news commentators were excitedly discussing the tragedy that had occurred only minutes before. A United flight had just crashed one mile from the runway. *It was my flight!*

I knelt beside my bed, and as the faces of those whom I had seen aboard the plane came to mind, I prayed for any survivors. Then I raised my hands in gratitude toward heaven. "Thank You, Jesus, for Your divine protection."

God also protected me on many other occasions, proving His faithfulness to His own.

Supernatural Assistance

One particular trip to the Caribbean Islands would best be described as a comedy of errors. While awaiting the takeoff, I sat near a window and watched the ground attendants outside scurrying around performing their individual tasks. I glanced about and noticed a puddle of oil was forming on the runway beneath one of the two Lear jet engines.

I unbuckled my seat belt, scrambled to my feet, and made a mad dash to locate the pilot and mechanic to report the oil leak. They shrugged, dismissed it as minor, and suggested that I reboard.

Upon my insistence, however, they reluctantly decided to look at the engine. I followed them, fearing to leave until I knew something was being done. They raised the flaps to investigate the leak, and one of them accidently dropped a monkey wrench into the bowels of the engine. After fishing it out, they finally located and repaired the leaking oil line with a coat hanger. But other problems were discovered, and the airline finally cancelled the flight—to our great relief.

During that same trip, we had to carry on our crusade without our sound system, which made two round trips by itself to Rio de Janeiro.

Another example of divine intervention occurred on what I like to call the Miracle Holy Land Tour. In October, 1973, during the Yom Kippur war between Israel and Egypt, one hundred and twenty-four people left New York with Kash and me bound for Israel via Paris. All similar tours from the U.S. had been cancelled because of the war.

In Paris, we were to connect with a flight to Tel Aviv. We discovered, however, that all seventeen airlines flying out of Orley Field had also cancelled their flights to Israel because of the danger. For a while it appeared that we would be stranded in Paris along with about six hundred other Holy Land pilgrims.

Kash and I believed that God would help us. After alerting the tour agency in Tel Aviv of our plight, we waited. Not many hours had passed when I was called back to the ticket counter. The young Israeli ticket agent informed me that a special El Al jet had arrived to transport our group on a direct flight to Israel. Some of the tour groups in the airport were eventually routed through Turkey and Switzerland. Other disappointed travelers waited until flights back to the United States became available.

The El Al pilot made an all-instrument landing in total darkness, touching down in Tel Aviv during the blackout. A cheer went up from the passengers, not only in appreciation for the skill of the pilot but also in praise to the Lord for His protection. We knew being there was a miracle.

A cease-fire called between Israel and Egypt the very next day left us free to tour Israel without jeopardy. God had performed the impossible. Some of the tour members jokingly called it the "Ken Gaub and Kash Amburgy Cease-Fire."

We visited the sacred and historic sites of the Bible Land while Israeli television crews filmed our progress. Articles were written about us in the Jerusalem Post. By placing ourselves into the trust and protection of the Israeli government and continuing our tour in their time of crisis, we sparked new hope and lifted the morale of the people of Israel.

The evening before our tour left Israel, a banquet was arranged in honor of Kash and I. Moshie Kohl, then Minister of Tourism for the Israeli government, presented us with beautiful gold pins of appreciation for our continued interest in the nation of Israel.

The return flight to the United States was a wonderful time of sharing and rejoicing for the way God had blessed our Miracle Bible Land Tour.

I still encourage people to fly with us. "I know for sure that God won't let me crash!" I assure people. "You're safe as long as I'm on board."

We always pray about our trips and tours. God, who knows the future, can surely direct us in advance about when to go, where to go, and which plane to take. We always make sure we feel His peace when we carry through with plans to go somewhere. 1 Corinthians 14:33 states, "God is not the author of confusion, but of peace." And Proverbs 3:6 says, "In all thy ways acknowledge him, and he shall direct thy paths."

Obedience is important, but you can't obey unless you listen. John 10:27 says, "My sheep hear my voice, and I know them, and they follow me." If you listen to the voice of God, He will lead and guide you. 2 Thessalonians 3:3 says, "The Lord is faithful, who shall stablish you, and keep you from evil."

God *will* direct your life. Absolutely nothing happens by chance with God, and there are no dead ends. You did not just happen. You were not born into this world as a bad joke. God wanted you here, and He has direction for your life. But you have to hear the voice of the Shepherd. Listen and, as you hear His voice, follow Him.

Chapter Twenty-Two

BARS DO NOT A PRISON MAKE

The sounds reverberated from the lead guitar, a crescendo of wild applause rose, and over twenty thousand people stood and cheered. *Eternity Express* received a standing ovation as they performed at *JESUS 80*.

Following their last number, I stepped up to the microphone. "I never get nervous about *things,*" I told the crowd. "I just get excited about *God!* I even get excited about being excited. It's fun to serve God. He wants you to believe Him for the impossible. . . ."

The thrill of ministering to such a crowd was clouded by our inability to mingle with the people. A high security fence separated the platform from the huge throng. We acknowledged the final applause and left the stage. Then a lady thrust a pad and pencil through the fence and politely asked, "Can I have your autograph?"

"Can I have *yours?*" I returned.

Her eyes widened in quick surprise. "I don't sign autographs," she stammered.

"Why not?" I questioned.

"I'm not a celebrity," she returned. "You're

somebody special."

"*You're* somebody special, too," I replied reaching through the fence to touch her hand.

"You're kidding!" she said, unsure of my sincerity.

"No, I'm not. Here, let me have your autograph! Please!" I thrust the pad back into her hands.

She looked at me for a moment, then giggled and signed it with a flourish. I tore the sheet off, folded it, and put it in my pocket.

"Remember, you are somebody. You are important. I'm no more important than you."

Tears formed little rivulets down her cheeks. She reached through the fence and hugged me. "Wow! Think of that!" she said, grinning broadly.

Later, when our twin Silver Eagle buses were once again on the open road, I had time to reflect on the response the band had received at the great open-air meeting. The acceptance of their music and their growth in popularity had suddenly mushroomed. It had been several years since the formation of the band.

For years our children had blended their voices with Barb's and mine as the "Ken Gaub Family Singers." We had sung around the world and produced eight albums.

Nathan, our oldest son, had begun his ministry with us when he was only eighteen months old. When Barb and I played and sang, he would accompany us on a plastic ukulele. By five he had traded the uke for a banjo. At ten he played the bass guitar and soon progressed to the electric piano.

Dan also made his musical debut at an early age. At three he inherited Nathan's discarded uke. Before long he had included a toy trumpet. Later he accompanied us playing a shiny new ninety-eight cent drum from Woolworth's. At eight someone gave him his first electric guitar. Because of our mobile lifestyle, he managed only one week of formal training. But through constant practice and by listening to every technique and sound he heard, he soon mastered the electric guitar and developed a unique style of fingering that combined both lead and rhythm.

Becki, who had been a song leader since age three, shook a tambourine and later tried various other instruments. Both she and Barbara played the accordion. Having no real inclination to stay with a particular instrument, Becki mostly enjoyed singing solos.

When *Eternity Express,* now known as *Illustrator,* evolved, it created a vehicle for Nathan, Dan, and my younger brother, Mike, who liked a more contemporary musical sound. Mike had joined us for a six-week tour. that turned into fulltime. He became our drummer (in addition to playing the mandolin and guitar). The boys gained favorable responses from our crusade audiences and soon had a following.

Other members of the band were added, as well as musical spouses for the boys. The band became well-rounded with talented musicians devoted to gospel work.

Across America we saw many thousands of young people not being reached by "conventional" church music ministries. As a result, the band began to include contemporary music and literally became a Christian music group for non-Christians.

Today's youth listen to rock groups whose sophisticated musical equipment communicates their lifestyle of drugs, immorality, and rebellion. To create a more professional contemporary sound, we purchased new electronic sound equipment. The results were worth every cent. We saw thousands of young people respond to the old-time gospel message set to a contemporary rhythm.

Many testimonies resulted, such as the runaway 15-year-old boy about to commit suicide. Someone invited him to come hear our band. Their signing reached his soul, and he found the Lord as Savior.

The contemporary sound of the band also helped open new doors for us, and we rejoiced as the Lord supplied the grace to walk through them.

Cold Steel and Melting Hearts

After passing through four, heavy steel gates and having our equipment thoroughly searched by grim-faced prison guards, I knew we were not going to a Sunday school class. We had to carry our equipment by hand — almost three thousand pounds of it — down long, stark corridors of concrete block and steel bars. We were in the maximum security area of Walla Walla, Washington State Prison. Special permission had been granted by the warden for us to minister behind bars.

Our reception was anything but friendly as we entered the large recreation room where we would conduct the meeting. Several hundred male prisoners of every race milled about the room, eyeing us suspiciously as we set up our sound equipment. The girls were extremely nervous and self-conscious under the gaze of so many leering eyes. The prison definitely presented no church atmosphere.

The chaplain had expressed concern for our safety because of the prison's reputation for prisoner unrest. Just the day before, a small riot had erupted. Pipe bombs had been hidden in several cells, and a guard had his hands blown off trying to dismantle one of the explosives. We learned later that he had died. The chaplain wasn't sure the prisoners would respond to a gospel concert, but I wanted to help those men.

As soon as the band began to minister in song, the apprehension and tension eased. The band opened with an unusual lyric:

> Drinking whiskey from a paper cup,
> Drown your sorrows 'til you can't stand up,
> A broken needle in your purple veins, It is
> Jesus that you need. . . .

The message set to the contemporary beat, a beat to which these prisoners were accustomed, caught their attention. I observed their reaction as the group sang. The faces of men in the audience mirrored their lives. Eyes scowled with hate. Lips sneered in contempt. Identifying homosexuals was easy; nobody had any hidden emotions. They had ruined their lives and ended up here, and I could sense their bitterness and hopelessness.

A stifling haze of tobacco smoke hung in the air. Many prisoners sat puffing on cigarettes. Others sat with hats on or walked about irreverently during the singing.

Just before I got up to speak, I prayed silently, "God, I know these men are really rough characters. Most are here for life. But I know you see their hearts. It doesn't matter what a man looks like on the outside; deep inside they are just like everybody else who doesn't know Christ—lonely and desperately in need of the saving grace of Jesus. Help me to say something to help change their lives."

As our band sang their hearts out, hardened expressions softened, and a feeling of peace settled over the room. Some men stamped out their cigarettes, and others paused to pay closer attention.

Wearing jeans and a T-shirt, I didn't look much like a preacher. I had asked the chaplain beforehand not to introduce me as Rev. Gaub because I didn't want to lose the attention of the men before I got started. The importance of what I had to say could change their lives—forever.

"I didn't bring any records to sell here," I kidded, trying to win their confidence. "You all already have one. I'm not going to take an offering because I might not get my plate back. One time I passed a hat and lost the hat. I'm not here to condemn you—the jury has done that."

Many of them had forgotten how to laugh and smile, but they began to loosen a bit. I discussed the fact that their previous decisions in life had brought them to that place of imprisonment, and I talked about making new decisions and about serving God. "Life's answers are not found in bottles, needles, drugs, or whatever. Life's answers are found in taking Jesus Christ as your personal Savior," I stated. "I would like you to come forward and accept Him. If you don't have the strength to get up now and stand for Him while it is easy, you will never do it tomorrow when you have to face the other men in the prison."

What a thrill to see those men respond and come forward. We handed out large print Bibles until we ran out.

From that day, our prison ministry grew quickly, as wardens, pastors, chaplains, and inmates begged us to come. One of the services we offered was to accept collect calls from prisoners who were in need of spiritual counsel.

At the famous Cook County Jail in Chicago, Illinois, seven hundred of their prisoners attended our service. We were thrilled when hundreds stood in response to accept the Lord Jesus Christ as Savior.

In one prison, a young man came up to me after our performance. I was startled to hear him say, "Ken, I know who you are. You may not remember me. If only I had listened to you in my home church when I first heard you, I wouldn't be here today."

Since then, hundreds of prisoners have come to know the Lord. We have provided literature, Bibles, and tapes to thousands. At Christmas time, we give gifts to many who otherwise would not receive anything. Many are forgotten people.

Jesus stated that He came to set the captive free. (See Luke 4:18.) Psalm 27:10 says, "When my father and mother forsake me, then the Lord will take me up." I have met hundreds of prisoners who are free even though they live in a cell.

Jesus Christ never forgets anyone. He knows where you are, when and why you hurt, and what you need. He is waiting for you to come to Him so He can free you from whatever bondages you are in—whether it's prison, a bad habit, or an ungodly lifestyle. Turn to Him, and He will set you free. (See John 8:32.)

Chapter Twenty-Three

A BIG EIGHTEEN CENTS

"Hurry up, boys. We need to be on the move." The empty auditorium in Casper, Wyoming, resounded with a hollow ring. Only half an hour before, it had been filled with people.

Standing with Gary, I watched as Dan, Mark, and Daryl carried out the last load of equipment. Nathan was in the deserted lobby stacking the remaining boxes of albums and tapes.

Preparing to leave, Barbara had already boarded the buses. I could hear the droning of the Silver Eagle diesels through the open door.

Suddenly, someone spoke to me. Wondering where the voice had come from, I turned and looked into the pleasant face of a young man. A serene quality radiated about him.

"Ken," he said, "God wants me to tell you something."

I thought, "Oh, no! Here's one of those people who like to prophesy to people." Aloud, I said, "Really? Sure. Go ahead!"

"Ken, because you have helped others, millions of dollars are going to come your way someday. You will

161

go through some things, but money will flow like a fountain if you're faithful. So, don't worry!'' Smiling, he turned to leave.

I turned to Gary and whispered out of the side of my mouth, ''Gary, watch this guy. He's probably one of those guys who likes to be the center of attention. Watch him! I bet he goes out to Nathan now and prophesies to him.''

We both turned back to watch him and couldn't locate him. Doing a double take, I said, ''Where did he go? He couldn't have gotten out that quickly. He had to walk past all those rows of seats before he could get to the door.''

Knowing he had to pass Nathan, I made my way to the back. Gary followed me. I yelled, ''Hey, Nathan, where did that guy go?''

''What guy, Dad?'' Nathan replied. ''No one has been by here.''

Curiosity compelled me to look out into the street. He was nowhere to be seen.

''That's impossible!'' I stammered. Then I remembered the look on his face—the sweet glow I had ignored. ''He could have been an angel!'' I concluded.

As we finished loading the bus, we drove on to Colorado Springs, Colorado, for our next meeting. After the service was over, a sweet-looking, elderly lady came up and said, ''Mr. Gaub, God wants me to tell you something.''

I grabbed her by the arm, thinking, In case this is another angel, I want someone else to see her and get a picture.

She looked at her arm and then looked at me. I'm sure she restrained herself, attempting to be polite.

"Yes, what is it?" I asked, trying to remain calm.

"God told me to tell you that because you have helped others, millions of dollars are going to come your way. You will go through some things, but money will flow like a fountain someday if you are faithful. Don't worry!" she said.

Standing shock still, I squeezed her arm even tighter. When she grimaced, I realized what I was doing and relaxed my hold. But I wasn't about to let go.

She further stated, "You know, this same thing was told to you in Wyoming. I'm only confirming what was told to you there."

"How did you know we were in Wyoming?" I said. "It wasn't on our schedule."

"God told me," she smiled. As she moved to leave, I moved with her. She looked at me, with my hand still clutching her arm. "I need to get to the car. My family's waiting on me," she explained.

"I'll go with you," I told her.

A little surprised at the special attention, she patiently allowed me to escort her out of the church. Wondering if there really was a car or if it was an excuse to get away from me, I thought, "I hope someone sees me. If she really is an angel, I will have witnesses. I'm hanging on to her for sure."

I felt a little silly when she got into the car with several relatives. I waved good-bye, wondering at the unexpected prophecies.

As we headed toward Washington, D.C., for our meeting with Pastor Bennie Harris at the Christian Center in Alexandria, Virginia, I pleaded with God to talk with me during the whole trip.

"God, I love You. I know You love me. Look at all

the strange things and miracles that have happened to me during my lifetime. I know it could have only been You and Your miraculous intervention. I want to know You more. My heart is hungry for a deeper relationship than ever with You. Lord, are these things really going to happen to me as the angel said. I do want to have the means to keep on helping people." This was my lifelong dream.

Feeling God should speak to me personally, I grew annoyed. "God, You're always sending people to talk to me. Where are You? I want You to talk to me Yourself."

I pleaded, "I'll tell You what, God. You know my address. It's Box 1, Yakima, Washington 98907. You can write me a letter."

When at last we arrived in Alexandria, Virginia, my spirit was perturbed. I stayed in the bus while the boys set up our equipment. More than anything in the world, I wanted confirmation that God was aware of me.

I thought for a minute and then wrote on a three-by-five card:

> God, if all these people coming to me are for real and what they have been telling me is true, then have a man give me an offering tonight of eighteen cents. I want it to be three pennies and three nickles.
>
> Ken

Expectantly, I folded it, wrote "God" on the top, and stuck it in a little box on a corner table. I reasoned to myself as I rushed into the building, Anyone can give me twenty dollars, but what fool would give me eighteen cents, especially three pennies and three nickles.

After the service, I stood in the foyer thinking about the note I had written and wondering if God would answer. Self-pity consumed me.

Everyone had gone home except the pastor, his wife and children, and my crew. We were just about through packing our equipment when a man with tear-stained cheeks and red eyes strode through the door and walked over to me.

"Ken, I'm Dan Carter. I've been sitting in my car crying and praying for a half-hour. I know this sounds crazy, and I really feel like a fool doing this—but I've got to."

With a look of humiliation on his face, he reached for my hand. With his other hand he dropped some coins into mine.

I opened my hand, looked down, and wept as I counted the coins.

He said, "I'm sorry. I know this embarrasses you to receive such a small amount, but I really thought it was what God wanted me to do."

"No, wait!" I said. I turned to my son and said, "Dan, go to the bus and get a little card out of the box on the corner table. It's folded and addressed to God. Bring it here quickly."

Everyone stood looking at me wondering what I was doing. I could do nothing but cry. Barbara asked, "Ken, what's going on?"

I was too moved to speak.

Dan came back on the run and handed me the paper. I shook my head, "Son, you read it to these people. I can't."

When Dan had finished reading the short note, the others standing in the foyer were moved to tears by the realization that they had witnessed a miracle of God's love and concern.

The incident totally revolutionized the life of the man who gave me the eighteen cents. Every time the story has been told, miracles have taken place.

When the pastor spoke at our building dedication, he related the story. I taped the three nickles and the three pennies to the original letter to God and still have it in my office.

It reminds me that "funny things do happen" as we journey through this life — not only funny, but serious things and miracles. In the last few years, we have seen thousands of young people commit their lives to Jesus Christ through the efforts of *Youth Outreach Unlimited* — in prisons, high schools, auditoriums, and parks. It has grown to a world wide ministry.

God has helped me to use humor to break down barriers that many people have and to portray the real truth about what the right kind of living can do. We praise God for miracles. Many people are listening and responding to the gospel message of love and hope.

The band's contemporary songs and personal witness lets young people see that their answers are not found in escaping reality with drugs, booze, and immorality. Answers are not found in bottles, needles, fame, or money but in knowing Jesus Christ as their Lord and Savior. Many people come to our appearances just to see what we're all about, and thousands of lives are turning to Jesus Christ. God has a miracle for everyone.

So, **WHEN YOU LEAST EXPECT IT, EXPECT IT!**